EDWARD AND VICTORIA

EDWARD
and
VICTORIA

URSULA BLOOM

ROBERT HALE · LONDON

© *Ursula Bloom* 1977
First published in Great Britain 1977

ISBN 0 7091 5909 9

Robert Hale Limited
Clerkenwell House
Clerkenwell Green
London EC1

Filmset by
Specialised Offset Services Ltd., Liverpool
Printed in Great Britain by
Lowe & Brydone Ltd.
Thetford, Norfolk

Contents

Illustrations

Foreword

I have a very deep admiration for King Edward VII whom I met at Warwick Castle when I was about five years old. My father was staying there during the week, and, being a parson, he had to go back to take services at home on the Sundays. He was helping Lady Warwick write *Warwick Castle and Its Earls*. He did all the research for her. I went with him one week, and was playing in the garden with her second son, Maynard Greville, when a bearded old gentleman came to us and gave us half-a-crown. I had never seen so much money before! He said, "You two slip out and get yourselves some sweets, and don't come home until you have eaten the lot, because if you do they will only take them away from you."

He was so right there, but, in those days, half-a-crown went a very long way, and I shall never forget how sick I felt afterwards.

That was the only time that I ever met the King.

U.B.

Introduction

When on a June morning in 1837, the young Princess Victoria was called to come down the staircase of Kensington Palace at dawn to meet the two men who had come to tell her that she was the Queen of England, she was just eighteen years old.

The reign of the feckless Georges had not been good for the country. It may have been a good time for the rich, but a very bad time indeed for the poor. The country was in a dreadful state, approaching bankruptcy, the money had trickled away.

The girl knew that one day she might be Queen, but probably she did not appreciate quite what it meant. She had been brought up in relative penury, for her mother, the Duchess of Kent, had only a small allowance, and was almost ostracized by other members of the Royal Family, who had never liked her. Victoria had been educated in the airy-fairy manner of the times, when the upper class thought it quite unnecessary to waste money on schooling a daughter who might marry money and live happily ever after! The widowed Duchess of Kent had been kept very short indeed, for the Georges, so generous to themselves, were extremely mean towards other people. The poor Duchess had hoped that things would improve when King George IV died and his brother William IV came to the throne, but nothing worked out too well for her. King George IV had made the most of his money whilst he had it, and now there was very little left.

Victoria had met few children of her own age because her mother had never invited little friends to the palace. It was necessary to live the simple life, and this was all that she could afford. Kensington then was a rural village; one told the time by the lowing of cows going out to pasture, or coming home to be milked! Anyway, the palace stood far from the road, away from everyone and everything.

It was her mother who awakened the Princess on that summer morning (the Duchess of Kent had been called by a maidservant saying, "two gentlemen are here"), and she went to rouse her daughter, her heart fluttering. She realized this was the hour! She said nothing to her daughter, only that she was wanted, and they went downstairs together to the carved door of the room where the Archbishop of Canterbury and the Lord Chamberlain were awaiting her. The Duchess would have gone into the room with her daughter, but she was stopped. Instinctively she knew then that she would walk behind her daughter from then on!

Victoria was entirely different from the Georges. There was far more of her Coburg mother in her than of her father; a quiet girl, though not shy, and in perfect health, for she had never had a week in bed in her life. At this time she was very slim, with auburn hair, a bright colour, and the light brows and eyelashes which go with the hair. She had that bright pink and white skin which comes with auburn hair, and she had also that glorious first flush of youth which has a beauty of its own and is so very attractive.

She had met George IV, whom she called 'Uncle George', about four times in her life, sufficient to prove to her that she did not like him. When he died and she visited the new King, whom she had known as 'Uncle William', she found him and his wife, Aunt Adelaide, much kinder to her, although they had never been effusive. There was nothing intimate about the relationship, because the Royal Family had never had much room for the Duchess of Kent, and therefore had not been encouraging to her or her little daughter. The Duchess, of course, was more of the *Hausfrau* type, rather prim (which none of them was), and it was so maddening that she had a living child, when they had not. King George had lost his daughter Charlotte when her dead son was born, and both the little daughters of King William died in infancy.

Victoria had liked her half-brother and half-sister, Feodora, the two children of her mother's first marriage, though as she grew older she saw less and less of her half-brother, Charles, for he ultimately returned to live in Germany.

When Princess Charlotte had died in 1817, to be buried at Windsor with her dead son in her arms, her father the Regent had panicked. He had thought that the succession to the throne was secure; and never for a moment had he thought of the Princess Charlotte dying. Thus he sent for his three younger surviving brothers (he was going to be quite sure of doing the right thing this time), and informed them that each must marry immediately, so as to provide an heir to the throne.

The brothers – the Dukes of Clarence (William), Kent (Edward) and Cambridge (Adolphus) – were *horrified*.

They were living quite happily with their mistresses (after the royal fashion of the time), and they had no wish to cast them aside and marry some princess as ordered by the Regent. But no loyal subject can say "No" to a royal edict of this kind.

The Duke of Kent had abandoned his mistress – his 'old French lady', Madame de St Laurent – and a large number of children (nobody seems to know what happened to them), and he had gone to Germany and had married the good lady who had been found for him. She was the widow of Emich, Prince of Leiningen, and was not even very attractive, but the King had commanded it and the Duke had to obey.

He had been rewarded, for he had the good fortune to sire a sturdy little daughter, heir to the throne of England provided everything went well.

Victoria could not remember her father; he had died before she could talk, and when she could only just toddle. She lived quietly with her widowed mother, because the income was insufficient to provide more than the plainest food and a few servants in Kensington Palace.

Victoria, although the childless King and Queen were

devoted to her, was kept very much in the background; the family's dislike of her mother meant that they asked her out only when they had to. She had been educated along the narrowest lines, learning practically nothing; this was not the era when girls ever learnt very much.

On that June morning, when the larks were singing their exuberant song to the new day, this great historical event took place. Others had seen it coming, but not a word of it had been conveyed to the young girl, brought up in the greatest simplicity, and she had been taught to ask no questions.

I do not think that her Mama had been a very affectionate woman, for she had lost her first husband, who had been a stern man, and then had been bustled into the second marriage with the English royal duke. She had married Kent out of a sense of duty and had settled in England only to find that her new relatives-in-law did not really care for her, and that her second husband, too, was very stern. Then she had been worried that her third baby was a daughter when the country so much wanted a son: widowed again, she did not taste the riches that she had always been told would be hers in England. She was given a suite in the palace, but was treated in such a way that she could be excused from concluding that her second marriage (which had sounded as if it was going to be so good) was very little better than her first one had been!

After Kent's untimely death she ran the home, saw that the child was taught a mere fraction of the lessons that she should have learnt, and was pleased when, on that June morning, when the sweet-smelling cowslips sparkled in the grass, she learned that King William IV had followed his brothers to rest.

That day the young girl's life changed completely.

She wept for Uncle William, who had always "been nice to her", though very little more, but she had shed no tears for Uncle George, whom she remembered visiting at Brighthelmstone, thinking him "very old indeed", and who had driven with her beside him in a grand carriage and had made the irritating remark, "Give me your little paw" when he shook hands.

She very much resented her own hand being called a 'paw'. Animals had paws, people did *not*.

On the whole she – possibly under her mother's influence – had not been too happy with her dead father's family, and she knew none of her mother's relations. Now had come that bright summer morning when the last of the Hanoverians had died.

The new Queen of England moved into Buckingham Palace the first moment that was possible, Mama with her. Then she found that she herself had changed very much in a short space of time. Until her accession, she had been a quietly obedient girl who had always done what she was told, and on the face of things appeared to enjoy doing it. Suddenly she had become the Queen of England, and, accepting her new position, quite suddenly she grew up. That very day itself at Kensington Palace she had asked that her bed be taken out of her mother's room, (where she had always slept), into one of her own.

She *was* the Queen now, and the Queen gave commands.

She had never thought her elevation would involve such a lot of work, for now there were always people waiting for an audience, ministers, with matters of urgency to discuss, and all sorts of commitments to be made. Her time had to be given up to people whom she had never seen before, and on the most demanding business, much of which she could not understand.

Things were explained to her, but not by her mother, her mother was no longer the dominant figure in her life. Men advised her, much older, wiser men, and they even helped her to understand what they were talking about. In particular she accepted the guidance of Baron Christian von Stockmar and of his royal mentor, Vicky's uncle, the future King Leopold of the Belgians.

In Buckingham Palace her first reaction was, "But there is such a terrible lot to learn!" She made up her mind to do the right thing; she had much of her father's determination; and she realized how little she knew and that, whatever happened, she had got to learn a very great deal at a time in her life when most girls come out into the world and choose a husband.

Life at Kensington had been eventless, but life in Buckingham Palace and at Windsor was the very opposite of that. She had not always been too happy as a child, for Mama had ruled her with a rod of iron. Now Mama had to do what *she* was told, and her daughter did not see too much of her. There was an unending lot of work to be done.

Gone now was the sheltered life, when she had had to wear a pinafore for a whole week because washing it cost money; when one could have only a small slice of cake for tea because to eat more would be extravagant; and when, at all costs, any waste of money must be avoided. Whenever she had asked as a hungry child why they had to retrench, as she often did, she had been told that it was the fault of Uncle George, the King.

She knew, of course, that she would have to marry, for an heir to the throne must be provided. The facts of life were kept from 'nice' girls in those days, and, unless they picked up some promiscuous confidences from one of the maids, they went into marriage with no idea of its meaning. But Victoria *did* know, for her mother had been honourable about this. She would have to bear a child, and pray that it was a prince, who could succeed her one day as King, and therefore she would have to find a suitable husband.

Until she ascended the throne Victoria had hardly ever gone out and about, but had played in the gardens of Kensington Palace, or in her nursery with her dolls. They never went into London, for her mother strove to conceal their poverty from the world, and few visitors came to see them for the very same reason, until it was obvious that she would succeed Uncle William.

For economy reasons the coronation was then not such an extensive ceremony as it is today and the service was not so long. Victoria returned to the palace, and after tea she washed her dog. It was as simple as that!

She had always been an extremely brave girl, and had come

to the palace with resolutions that she would make the country happier under her reign, ruling it ably and well. She sought to help the poor.

At that time the under-privileged classes were indeed poor; people were going barefoot in the streets, dying in the winters, and last century at this time there were some very cruel winters. She would not be extravagant herself. Her advisers were surprised how she wished to learn all details of where she could check expenses, and how she could do without.

"I have got to change so much," she told herself.

She accepted her new position extremely seriously. She had been educated on the principle of being 'seen and not heard'. She realized very soon after she became Queen that she had a lot to learn, and she determined that in future she would be heard as well as seen.

When the two young German princes – Ernest and his brother Albert of Saxe-Coburg and Gotham came on a visit to her at Windsor Castle she knew before they actually met that, if she liked one of them, he could be the most suitable husband for her. It was her first Prime Minister, Lord Melbourne, who had told her this very guardedly, for it was difficult to make the direct suggestion that she should choose one of them.

She could speak fluent German, but to her surprise she found that they both spoke very good English! They dined together, and she was happier than she had thought they would be. That night the carpets were rolled back, and they danced, which delighted her.

Next day they rode in Windsor Great Park. Vicky rode very well. This was the first time that she had entertained young men of her own age, and she found that she was enjoying their society greatly.

However, she thought that Prince Ernest was a 'know-all'; he was, in truth, a rather conceited young man, and quite sure of the position which he would hold in this country if he married the Queen. Prince Albert was the quieter and the more natural and unaffected of the brothers. He was sure that

Ernest was going to be the Queen's bridegroom, and he had come with him chiefly because he was very interested in England as a country and wanted to see it for himself.

He teased her quite a lot. Nearer her age, and with nothing to worry about (Prince Ernest by contrast was pompous and rather starchy) the younger prince could relax and be himself! Albert decided that Windsor Great Park was glorious, that the girl rode very well, and that he liked the colour of her hair.

He was a tall young man, extremely good-looking, and he carried himself very well. He amused the girl. Since she had become Queen nobody had tried to make her laugh! He could do this — and did! In a way he felt sorry for her; she was so young, so inexperienced, and he realized that she knew very little about the hard work of being a Queen.

Prince Albert himself had had the most remarkable education in Coburg. He adored learning and was a first-class scholar, whilst the education of the little Queen had been quite the poorest that she could have had. He pitied her.

His brother Ernest in his conceit determined to give the best possible impression of himself and show that he knew everything, but Albert, the scholar, did not trouble. It was Ernest who felt perfectly sure that *he* would marry the Queen.

The decision, of course, lay with her, and ultimately Victoria sent for the younger of the two brothers. She received him in her private drawing-room at Windsor Castle. She asked him if he understood how the country felt about this visit of the two young princes. The country wished her to wed. Would this make him happy? Possibly her manner betrayed the truth, for she was very young, and already she was most deeply in love with him.

Albert showed no confusion, though apparently her decision was entirely unexpected, for all the time he had been told that Ernest was destined to be the Queen's bridegroom. She told him that because she was the Queen she *must* wed, and if this would make him content, then she would be very happy herself.

He kissed her hand dutifully, but no one will ever know

what his emotions were. Undoubtedly he entranced her. Later she said that he was the first man who had argued with her since she had become Queen, and that could have attracted her. He was glamorous, with startling good looks, and his brilliant education was to be of the utmost benefit to her during the first quarter-century of her reign. In fact it was Albert who made Victoria so great.

They were married in the Chapel Royal at St James's Palace on 10th February 1840.

Their first child was a daughter, the Princess Royal who was to become the ill-fated Empress of Germany and to bring into the world the son who would become Wilhelm II, to whom England owes absolutely nothing except the ruin of many of her hopes.

When the Princess Royal was a few minutes old the Prince tiptoed into the room to see the Queen. She was very brave (thankful it was over, of course) and she apologized for giving him a daughter, but with great courage she reassured her husband that next time it would be a Prince of Wales, the heir whom her country wanted so much.

She was dead right in her forecast, for the next baby *was* the Prince of Wales. He was born at twelve minutes to eleven o'clock on the morning of 9th November 1841, coming into this world in the same bedroom where his elder sister had been born.

"A boy! A prince!" said Mrs Lily, the midwife who had attended the Queen during the lying-in. She is credited with having told the Duke of Wellington that the new arrival was a prince, not just a boy.

The Queen, exhausted after a "very severe" childbirth, murmured: "I do thank God for a Prince of Wales," – which the infant son was created in his cradle.

1

A Growing Family

The Queen's diary, which she kept most faithfully to her dying day reported that her first son was born at the very moment when the guard was changing at the palace. She added:

> I don't know what I should have done, but for the great comfort and support that my beloved Albert gave me.

Mrs Lily was enchanted; from the first she had predicted that this would be a son, and there was something very knowledgeable about these old-time midwives. She had had no training whatsoever, of course, but her mother had "done it before her", and she had picked up her knowledge from the old lady. No baby was weighed (that did not seem to worry them) and, of course, hygiene was unknown, but somehow or other they got through.

The previous November night, with a little fog hanging over the palace, a carriage and pair had crashed out of the gate from the royal stables, travelling at speed to the meadows where Mrs Lily's cottage stood: today those meadows are buried beneath Victoria railway station.

The prince was born into an age when it was the custom on the birth of an heir to the throne for the Captain of the Guard on duty outside the palace to be promoted Major. The prince arrived at the precise moment when the guards changed, and the new Captain and the departing one both claimed the promotion. In the end I believe they argued it out, but I do not know who won.

The Queen's diary noted that her son was born on the morning of Lord Mayor's Day. Oh, how thankful she must have been! As soon as ever she could, gallant little Mrs Lily whisked herself into a clean apron (she had brought a large parcel of 'pinnies' with her) and then went out into the ante-room to convey the good news to the gentlemen who were waiting for it.

The baby was well made, a big boy, and had come into this world with as much fuss as possible. There were no anaesthetics in those days (as yet chloroform had not been thought of) and everybody thought it quite usual to have a baby – that was what women had been created *for*!

In her diary the Queen wrote:

> Then Albert brought in dearest little Pussy [the pet name given to their daughter] in such a smart white merino dress, trimmed with blue, and a pretty cap, which Mamma gave her. He placed her on my bed, and she was so dear and good. And, as my precious invaluable Albert sat there, our little love between us, I felt quite touched with his happiness and gratitude to God.

The Queen was a most devout woman, and I think that she felt that she had disappointed her people in not having had a son for her first child. Now she had atoned for that. The boy was born the Duke of Cornwall, the title that comes into the world with a Prince of Wales, who can be created at any time thereafter. He was a fine, healthy child.

Queen Victoria was a born mother in the era of the large family. She had no wish for her throne to go back to the Georges (who had made such a mess of things), and knew it was important that she should have sons and daughters ready to take over when the hour came. She had now got two children to make the line secure. The country had great faith in her: she was the Queen who did the *right* thing, where they had been used to Kings who invariably did the *wrong* thing. She was determined that this little prince would be educated as an English prince should be.

"I want him to be like Albert," she said.

He was destined to inherit – although he did not necessarily make use of – his father's great brains. Most certainly he had his father's courage, and some of his mother's also, for undoubtedly the Queen *was* a very brave woman. He was baptized at St George's Chapel, Windsor, on 25th January 1842, and he received the names of Albert Edward. The baptism of the King destined to be 'the Peacemaker' coincided with a time of great unrest in Europe. There was the greatest difficulty to find anyone at all illustrious enough to become his godfather. In the end King Frederick William of Prussia consented to accept the honour, but he first consulted Prince Metternich, the Austrian Minister, before he finally said "Yes". It was the Duchess of Buccleugh who laid him in the arms of the Archbishop of Canterbury to be baptized.

He wore, of course, the magnificent Honiton lace baptismal robe, which had been made for his elder sister's baptism before she came into the world. To this day all the royal babies have been baptized in this robe. Today it is cared for, and treated very gently, because it is growing frail; and how it has been preserved so well for so long I cannot imagine.

All the royal children were of German origin on both sides, and very much cut to pattern, when it came to their manners and good behaviour.

They were brought up far more strictly than children are brought up today. They were frequently punished and given a good whipping, which was supposed to be the right thing to do, and they never spoke unless spoken to. Nearly all good families kept their children in the background, but Queen Victoria was anxious to have hers with her as much as possible, and she took them about with her to get used to the public.

She also knew that people wished to see them, and felt that, as the country paid for the upkeep of the Royal Family, they had a perfect right to see what they were paying for.

Well-bred children of the early Victorian era were perhaps allowed to come downstairs after tea for half an hour, but not always that. The Prince agreed with Victoria that people had a right to see her children. Albert thought that the younger they learnt the royal formula the better it would be for them. She herself had received no preparation for the throne, and it had meant a gruelling amount of work when ultimately she found what was expected of her.

"These children cannot learn too soon," her husband said, and rightly.

Because of her own strange upbringing, the Queen had found her personal shyness a great hindrance when she had first come to the throne. It had taken far too long to get accustomed to the demands of her high estate, of learning things that she should have learnt before she was twelve years old; this was not going to happen to her own children, she decided.

Victoria was grateful to Albert for explaining how wrong it had all been. She appreciated his comfort and his tremendous aid.

He trained her step by step; at first she was against it and protested, and he let her make bad mistakes twice just to show her that she did *not* know. In the end she was his pupil as well as wife.

After the Prince of Wales was born she wrote to a friend:

You will understand how fervent are my prayers, and I am sure that everybody else's must be, to see him resemble his angelic father in every respect, both in body and mind. How happy I should be to see *him* grow up like *him*!

She was desperately in love with the Prince, even more than she had been on the day when they had married.

History has never managed to record exactly how the Prince felt about it. At first he must have been both lonely and unhappy in a strange country. He would have felt homesick for Germany, which could have given him far more than England at this time. Then, when he got to know his Queen better, and had proved to her that her education had been indifferent, he *did* find a new joy in teaching her the things that she did not know, and helping her become the greatest Queen of all.

He directed her. The country had been through a most

difficult time for too long, when the extravagant Georges were on the throne, and now had come the moment to change everything. He won the Queen over! She studied with him, and turned for his advice in all emergencies. The people discovered that these two very young people sought to do the best they possibly could for the country, and they slowly began to evoke the admiration of those over whom they reigned. They were solicitous for the poorest of the poor.

I doubt if the people then realized that the brain behind the throne was that of the Prince, and the splendid work he did when he helped her meet some of the shocking needs of the uneducated and neglected people.

The future Prince Consort had been shaken by their plight. At the beginning of Victoria's reign men and women in the East End of London could not afford shoes; they walked barefoot. Too often they died in the gutter. Cleanliness was something that nobody concerned themselves about.

The Prince got over his home-sickness when he started to teach Victoria how to reign, and how to set a good example to her country and really help the poor. He pointed out that they had to set an example to others beneath them. They must be kind, solicitous for their well-being, and comforting in their need. This was the message that Prince Albert sought to get over to the general public. It all took time, but he did it in the end.

He brought about the most amazing improvements. When he had toured London he had been shocked by the poverty and the cruelty brought to his attention.

"We have got to build a new future, Victoria," he told her.

"You will help me?" she asked, knowing that she never had to ask him twice.

He laid the foundation stones for that new future, not realizing probably that it would be a mighty empire. It would take time (and at first the job must have seemed to be impossible), but he was a man not easily daunted. He was always the inspiration of his doting wife.

England was at a low ebb when the Prince came to marry

the Queen. The palace looked magnificent, of course, but the slums were ghastly. It was nothing to see a dead man lying in a back alley. She would never have been able to cope with the situation alone. She had not the wisdom or the education. But the Prince stood behind her.

The Queen did not 'receive' during the month that she spent in bed after her son's birth, for this would have been considered rather dangerous. It was so strange to contrast the risks that they took, and apparently thought nothing of, with their exaggerated care when nothing much could have happened. It was not the era of good medicine, really.

She got up again, the child was baptized, and as soon as possible Victoria was pregnant again: she felt she had to supply sufficient heirs for the throne which, when she had come to it, was in a fairly perilous position. It was much more secure now.

The son and heir was to grow up to become the sort of young man of that period who enjoyed a bottle of champagne and a pretty woman – very much!

Prince Albert had never cared for drink, nor had he become agitated by a pretty woman, for as a zealous student he had been far too busy. Scholarship took pride of place! He loved learning, and to the end of his life he was always learning something new. He had been the most ardent student when in Germany, and, although he had married the young Queen of England, I am sure that it was not a case of love at first sight for him. I am also sure that he would have pitied her helplessness, and he must have realized how much his supreme knowledge and understanding of what was needed would help her through many a difficulty. These difficulties with time grew greater. He did not let them obscure his vision: he had designs for England. He was a man with bold ambitions, prepared to carry them through.

Undoubtedly Albert the Good was dedicated to duty, (it inspired him) and he was now the power behind the throne. At the same time, on the domestic scene, he tried to persuade her to be more friendly with her mother. The Duchess of Kent lived in the palace, but her daughter was too often far too busy to see her, and the Prince, educated to love his relations, was sorry for her and tried to make his wife relax towards her.

When the children came, the Prince (homesick for Germany) became happier. He felt that now he had a far more real interest in his adopted country. Married to its Queen, he had held the future King in his arms. A devotee to royal duty, he was prepared to fill his role exactingly. He was enchanted with his son. The little prince had a most infectious laugh, and merry blue eyes that twinkled when he was happy. They were very proud of him, and took the greatest interest in his upbringing.

He had, as a baby, the most lusty cry. He spent his first seven months of life in what was then called a bassinet, a cane Moses basket, with handles on either side, so that it could be carried around with the baby in it. These were used before cots were introduced. On gala days he lay in a wooden cradle, which could be rocked. He was closely guarded by day and by night, and he flourished in the pleasant nurseries of Buckingham Palace, nurses with him all the time. One whimper – and someone was at his side.

Pussy had been enchanted with her baby brother, and the following year a small sister arrived to keep the two of them company. This was Princess Alice, born in the spring of 1843. Having a baby had become part of the royal routine, for there must be surety ahead for the crown. Having another baby was almost an annual event, until in the end the nation became slightly vehement about the large family, complaining: "We are the people who had to support them, and this is going on for ever!"

The Queen set the fashion for large families, being well aware of how speedily even large families can die out. But she was furious when the country said that she had too many children for them to keep. She had come to a very lonely throne, and her anger can well be understood.

The throne had fallen into disrepute under the later

Hanoverians, for none of whom would she have given a brass farthing. Their views were entirely contrary to her own, their outlooks quite different.

The one thing she wanted to be sure of was that the throne did *not* return to 'the old Georges'. Their duty was to make it secure, Albert told her, and to make sure that there were sufficient heirs of their own to carry on. Nevertheless she resented the regular pattern of child-bearing, which often made her miserable.

The young Victoria had changed very much from the girl who had come to Buckingham Palace, dismayed by the urgent demands made upon her, and she had been at a loss until she had married. She was amazingly surprised at the range and scope of her husband's knowledge, and although there were moments when he had put her right, and she had turned with the words, "Leave me alone. I *am* the Queen, and have the right to go my own way," in the end that changed. She found that he knew better than she did, and was guided by him. She became humbler and more grateful for his tuition.

Her husband was anxious because so often Victoria privately entertained the wrong feelings about people, and would not unbend. She was often entirely wrong, but would not change her mind. He tried to break her of this habit. For instance, she nursed a very strong resentment against King George IV, and carried it with her to her grave. It seemed that she jumped to conclusions, forming a liking or dislike too quickly, and then obstinately refusing to change a mind that was already made up.

"It is no help to dislike people," he told her; "far better learn to like them."

Possibly she knew that her husband was right, but somehow she always disliked some people. Just the same as her husband disliked the way that she behaved to her mother. At heart, Victoria had never really liked the Duchess, and now they met as seldom as she could contrive, although her husband made the most gallant attempts to change her attitude. The Duchess loved her grandchildren, but if ever

Victoria could prevent her seeing them she did so.

"I form my own conclusions," she told him.

"People are not always right in this," the Prince said. "It does not make you happier to nurse a grievance. It cannot help you to dislike someone! I wish I could persuade you. My aim is to make life easier for you."

She changed the decor at the palaces and now they were well furnished and clean. In the old days they had been neither. She was fundamentally very just, and staunch in her duty. She sought her husband's advice when she was uncertain of a decision and, as the family grew, she trusted him implicitly.

But this more relaxed outlook never applied to her eldest son, and it was a great anxiety to his father. She believed she should train all her children to cope with crowds; they were not to be shy. Once, when her husband suggested that her eldest son was a little young for this training, Victoria turned on him. She said rather sternly: "I was never trained at all in any way. I was quite unused to crowds, and people, and places. I have had to learn, and I would not want any child of mine to go through that same suffering. A royal child has to be a royal child, and the sooner they get accustomed to it, the better it is for their future."

Most certainly she trained all her children magnificently, though she came to be far more lenient with her youngest son, Prince Leopold. All his life he had to be guarded, and cared for, because of this wretched 'bleeding' that his nurses feared so much. He was taught to be far more careful than the others, and never to take risks, but there were times when privately she was very worried for him. But she presented the nation with the picture of a happy home and a wonderful marriage for love. Yet at heart, deep down within herself, it was her eldest son who always caused her the most heart-searching.

In fact, she was more anxious for Prince Edward than she was for Prince Leopold! It was so urgent to be sure that Albert Edward would make a good King, to be certain that he studied hard enough, and knew what to do. She herself had suffered for her haphazard upbringing, and for this reason felt all the more concerned for her own heir. One thing made *her* thankful: after he was four years of age his likeness to George IV seemed to fade, and she did not notice it so much. He was a child who liked fun, common to his age group; in this he was very like George IV who had got into a lot of trouble playing pranks in the lanes of Brighthelmstone long after dark when hard-working, early-rising workers did not wish to be disturbed by a King playing silly pranks in their immediate vicinity.

The Queen saw to it that her eldest son did his lessons rigorously. After a time, the world noticed this, and complained. *Punch* in particular had a word or two about what they called "high-pressure teaching", and they must have been very near to the truth.

His father agreed with the Queen's methods; in fact they had mapped out the rules together. It was difficult, for Albert had always delighted in learning, and appreciated nothing better than a day of strenuous study. He could not understand how children found learning boring, and the school rooms in the palace were, he knew, extremely demanding. They had to be, for royal children cover a greater field of lessons than is required of commoners.

The first governess to the little Prince was Lady Lyttleton, who taught him how to read and write when he was very young. She told his parents that he was a promising pupil, and he found very little difficulty in this, although arithmetic was not his strong point. He was very fond of Lady Lyttleton, who was kind and helpful, and guided him around the difficult corners.

2

Trials and Travels

The time came when, growing past babyhood, and the era of the very little child, Albert Edward would have to be under a highly-trained tutor to open his mind to that vast flow of constitutional and general knowledge which is so necessary for a future King. When he knew that Lady Lyttleton must leave him he was shattered. He would, she told him, have someone much cleverer to instruct him than she could ever be. He burst into tears! She explained that the time had come when his parents thought that he would be better with a man to teach him than a woman. He did not agree with any of this, and implored her not to desert him. He was a most tender-hearted, sweet little child who very easily became deeply attached to people.

His first principal tutor was the thirty-year-old Mr Henry Birch, who diagnosed that the little boy had an aptness for study above the normal for his years. This pleased the Prince Consort, but the Queen, ever dubious about this son of hers, had the idea that somehow or other he had got round his new tutor – a former Eton master – and persuaded him he was far cleverer than he really was. She queried everything that her eldest son did, or what he said. Perhaps she had always expected too much of him. It rather looked like it.

But he and Mr Birch liked one another, and he was happy with his new master. The Prince was a very merry little boy and the echo of his laughter rang through the royal nurseries. Tutors and pupil rose at eight, and went to bed at six, until the Prince was nine, then at half past six, gradually growing a little later.

In the end Mr Birch took Holy Orders and resigned. He had had his differences with Prince Albert, who did not agree that young Bertie should have more contact with boys of his own age. But the pupil had grown very fond of his teacher after the boy had learned to curb his natural impertinence and disobedience, and when he learnt that Mr Birch was leaving him he burst into tears and said that he could not bear to part with him. A lady of the Court wrote of this episode:

> Mr Birch left yesterday. It has been a terrible day for the Prince of Wales, who has done no end of touching things since he heard that he was to lose him, three weeks ago. He is such an affectionate, dear little boy. The notes and presents which Mr Birch used to find under his pillow were really too moving. ...

In succession to Birch the Prince Consort engaged Frederick Waymouth Gibbs, an amiable tutor, to take Mr Birch's place, and the child also turned to him with real affection. It was *Punch* which published the merry verse which is anything but a great verse (how it got into the paper as it was amazes me, for one would have thought that it really ought to have been vigorously edited.)

> Poor little Wales, sure the saddest of tales
> Is the tale of the studies with which they are cramming thee.
> In thy tucker and bibs, handed over to Gibbs,
> Who for eight solid years with instruction was cramming thee!

The Queen was most indignant when she saw it, as she always chafed against criticism of any kind because she felt that the Royal Family could do no wrong! She had developed a far more forceful personality, and, under the tender teaching of her Prince, she had become more knowledgeable and more commanding over matters on which she had to come to a decision.

Growing beyond that gay, girlish youthfulness in which she had come so radiantly to the throne, she was now able to lay down the law. She was absolutely furious when John Leech designed a cartoon which showed the Prince of Wales on a rocking-horse, with the British lion trotting along behind him, and underneath it the words – "You want Marlborough House, and some stables? Why, you'll be wanting the latchkey next, I suppose?"

The Queen felt that none of this was very funny, and that it should be stopped, for it happened at a time when the young Prince was growing up, and she was trying to make up her mind if Marlborough House would be good for him when he *did* grow up, because it was near the palace. She was a woman who liked to plan arrangements far ahead, and then got very annoyed when something leaked out! She fumed when things went wrong, but her husband could manage her, and he always guided her most carefully through the difficulties of royal life. When truly worried she would write for counsel to her uncle Leopold, the King of the Belgians (a marvellous counsellor, whose often sage advice saved her from making mistakes, many a time).

She would *not* be criticized, and said so repeatedly. She asked the King of the Belgians, if she ought to ignore this, or attack it? The King was a placid man; his rule was that it was always better to let things pass than to come out into open battle with the Press. Unless it was a scandal that was devastating to the Sovereign, she should rise above taking notice of it.

Victoria had been very clever in the way that she had got each of her children accustomed to crowds, and taught them not to be shy. This came when they were very young indeed. At this time in her life, it seemed that more and more babies were arriving at the palace, for she was making sure of the succession.

Bertie was never shy by nature, and could enter into anything that was going on around him. At the baptism of Prince Alfred, he had become very interested in a wig that the Archbishop of Canterbury was wearing and was so fascinated by it that he could not take his eyes off it! In the end, when the service was over, and he could hold back no longer, he approached the Archbishop.

"What is that thing on your head?" he asked. "It is not a hat, or a cap. What is it?"

"It is a wig!" the Archbishop told him, none too pleased.

"Do you take it off to ladies?" the child asked, and the Archbishop said shortly that he did *not*!

Conforming to the fashion of the age, the young Prince wore a girlish frock until he was six years old, then he went into sailor suits, which brought every other little high-class boy in England into the same uniform. The Queen's children led the fashions for the young. When she thought of her own youth, alone in Kensington Palace, learning little and doing nothing, she felt that her family had got the greater chances, and only hoped that all would turn out well.

The children were always friendly (she was most insistent about this) and never shy. Also quite early they learnt how to treat the crowds, to be pleasant, but not too familiar, and respond amiably to the waves and the cheers.

The Queen's last child was the infant Princess Beatrice, who, in the end, turned out to be her mother's favourite child when she lived at Osborne, waiting for her call to come.

As I have said Victoria flared up when people criticized her. After all, her sole thought was for the country, and the aid that she had given to it was far better than that of any of her predecessors.

When he grew up her eldest son told her: "Talk dies. Never concern yourself too much with it, for it comes and it goes."

"It is wrong to criticize one's ruler," she told him. "One day when you reign, you may feel the same way yourself."

In those future years of his brief reign, most certainly he felt the rasp of sharp tongues, and the criticisms which pursued him, and, like his mother, he was hurt by it!

Victoria always told herself how fortunate she had been in marrying a most brilliant man (possibly the cleverest in the world, at that time), for he had guided her to make the nation great. They worked together, giving of their best, as they prayed their son would do later, when his hour came.

"He has so much to learn!" his mother said, rather sadly.

"He has to start young because there is everything lying before him, and, whatever happens, he must be properly prepared to accept it. I know how ignorant I was myself, when I became the Queen, and how hard it was, and the difficulties in which I found myself. Whatever happens, that must *not* happen to him!"

She was very right there, although it is possible that her son did not think so. He had a very quick brain, inherited from his father, and learning would have come more easily to him but for the tough regimen to which he was subjected, leaving him with little time to do more exciting things. He worked far too long hours for any boy (*Punch* had been right about that one) and there seemed to be no end to the lessons that he had to learn at Albert's direction. Mercifully he had inherited his father's brilliant memory, and there was practically nothing that he read that he forgot afterwards. The memory stayed with him.

Like most other boys of his age, quite naturally he disliked lessons, and the Queen admitted that he had to do more than others, for that is the toll of kingship. The method of the teaching of that time was that, if a boy disliked it, you gave him more to do! Always his mother wanted to know how he was progressing, only too anxious that he should be a good King, and not as wretchedly ignorant as she had been. She said she would never have managed save for the wonderful tuition that her husband had given her. She would have been lost without him.

From the very early days when he had started learning with his governess, the young Prince reckoned that he had to do much more than other boys. Learning was a driving force behind him. He was angry that he had to learn more than his brothers and sisters, but he *had* been blessed with this very good memory, and undoubtedly it helped him enormously.

She brooked no argument with people who resented her behaviour to her eldest son, and still worried that he had inherited much from George IV who had been the bane of her own and her mother's life. He should never have been born, she always said. Most certainly he had let the crown down, and she believed, very nobly, that it was her duty to bring it back to its proper position. She knew what *Ich Dien* meant, and most certainly she *did* serve.

Her son was twelve when the Crimean War came, horrifying the world and the whole of Europe with the most appalling accounts of suffering, which came back from the front.

I am sure that many of the most horrible tales were told in front of this child when he was at a most impressionable age, and thus germinated his sheer horror of war, a horror that he never lost. He sought to prevent wars; to do something so that they could never come and to be the greatest peacemaker in the world, and this was the resolution that he took to the Stone of Scone in the hour when he was crowned to become Edward, the Peacemaker.

As he grew older he came to realize his own important position in this world and the urgency of the need to exercise benevolent power. He realized now why his teaching had been so important. He was utterly devoted to his father, the most charming man, who on the whole guided the boy very cleverly, and who led him into a more reasonable attitude towards his lessons. His mother was always rather stern with him (they never got on together as she did with her other children), and he regretted this, sometimes bitterly.

There was really no reason at all why she should have had the cool feelings that she did have towards her eldest son, for his tutors told her that he was a good scholar, save that, like all boys, his harassed mind wandered off at times, but that was nothing.

From the age of ten it was thought by Mr Gibbs that it would perhaps be a very good idea if some boys of his own age came over from Eton College to study with Bertie occasionally. He needed competition, and the tutor felt that he would work far better under competitive conditions. Some of the boys at Eton would come over and have tea with him at Windsor, and discuss their lessons together.

The boys selected went through a form of 'prep', which was a great help. It also checked some of the signs of reserve that the Prince had been showing, for he was at a difficult stage of his development, and shyness must be stopped. A shy king is impossible, his tutor told him, and whatever happened they must not allow *that*.

The new arrangement was a very good one, and after a few weeks, working with other boys, all traces of difference left him. He was a companionable boy who got on well with others and he found lessons shared to be far easier than they had been when he and his tutor had worked quietly together.

"It is right for him to meet as many boys of his own age as can be managed," his very efficient tutor said. "The whole of his adult life will be spent in meeting people, and still more people, talking to them and understanding them. He has to prepare for a life when he can take the initiative, and when he understands others."

Possibly the first real thrill of his life came when he was just fourteen years of age, a thrill that he was to remember throughout his time. It was the occasion when he fell in love with France!

The Queen and Prince Albert were playing a week's state visit to the French Court of Napoleon III and the Empress Eugénie. At the very last moment Queen Victoria got the sudden inspiration of taking with them the young Prince and his sister Pussy. When they were older, much of their lives would be spent travelling in foreign countries, and it would be helpful for them to go to France then, whilst they were still children (and excused, as children are) and it might be a stepping-stone into their future.

When they were told about it, they were greatly excited.

The young boy was impressed by everything he saw on this visit abroad to the country which he grew to love so much. It was the first time he had ever been abroad, and the French doted on him from the moment they saw him – in his tartan kilt – and his sister. "*Les enfants!*" they shrieked, when they saw the two elder children of the English Queen, standing by their father and mother. They were given a tremendous ovation. Even if the Prince of Wales was at the age when he very much resented being referred to as *"un enfant"*, the applause was so great that he could only smile to them, and wave back with the joyous approval of a young boy! He took it all in his stride.

He was enamoured of the French, their beauty, and by their abundant joyful spirit. He adored the gay life after his mother's quiet Court. Paris enchanted him.

This was possibly the moment when his great love for France was born, and the affection lasted through to the bitter end. *Toujours la belle France*!

He loved these gay people, he adored their music and the exciting dancing after the staid calm of reliable Victorian England. Here there was fun! He admitted that he lost his heart to the Empress Eugénie, a radiantly beautiful woman who spoilt him in a way that was never permitted at home, where his Mama always said "He *must* not have too much." Here he was overwhelmed with compliments and presents. Even when he went to bed the Empress sent him up sweets (treated as a sin at home, for his nannie would never allow a taste of anything after the teeth had been cleaned for the night).

"I love it here. It is all so beautiful," he said.

His parents, of course, were rather uneasy. All that impulsive gaiety, they felt could be part of the Georgian legacy, and privately they were suspicious of it. Here, staying in the French Court, Bertie was actually allowed to attend what he called 'grown-up parties'. His mother was horrified because, as she said, it was all wrong, he was far too young! The charming Empress helped him; he adored her. Possibly it was at this time, too, that his great love for beautiful women started. Eugénie never reproved him, whereas his mother was for ever finding fault. Victoria did love her children, but was always ready with a reprimand if they did anything of which she disapproved.

Bertie was very depressed when the time for leaving came.

The Empress comforted him.

"But, *chéri*, your mother could not do without you," she said, according to Greville's memoirs.

He answered, "Don't fancy that! They don't want us, and there are six more of us at home!"

She laughed at this frank sally, flinging back her pretty red head in the way that he so admired. She said that he would return to Paris when he grew up and was a man. He did, of course!

He dreamt for ever of the enjoyment there, the extreme beauty of the women, their lovely clothes, and the dancing to lively music. Getting back was a grind, for he could have stayed there happily for the rest of his life. London was prim, it had none of that joyous fun which the French call *joie de vivre*. London seemed sombre, the palace grim, and his parents were stern with him when he could not learn his lessons perfectly.

The Queen and his father were determined to make a sound and solid country out of the wreck it had been when they first started to rule, and Victoria was always afraid that the Hanoverian taste for slack living might leave some trace on her children; the one she suspected most was, of course, the Prince of Wales.

Possibly because of this fear she treated him more severely than she should. She found "no special pleasure or compensation in the company of the elder children" and only occasionally did she find "the rather intimate intercourse with them either easy or agreeable".

Bertie was an affectionate son. He also adored fun, but his mother was afraid of that "careless rapture" which had led her ancestors into folly. She and Albert worked hard and nobly to put England back on to its feet. Gradually things improved. The hour came when, in the country, you no longer saw the crude gallows on some country hillside, with a rotting, unrecognizable corpse swinging from it. New buildings were going up in London itself, impressive places of which a country could be proud, and Kensington grew to be part of

London. She had every reason to be happy with what she and her husband had done. Crime was lessened, life was more orderly, the impact of their mutual rule (for she owed all the really big moves to her husband) was beginning to make itself shown. She recognized that her eldest son was growing up into a fine boy, who had inherited some of her own good qualities and his father's handsome looks, which pleased her. But she meant to keep him under her thumb and it was only reluctantly that she allowed him to go on walking tours with tutors in Dorset and the Lake District and, when he was fifteen, to visit Germany "for the purposes of study", which he broke off temporarily to kiss a pretty girl.

Art interested the three elder children. Most of Queen Victoria's family liked painting and drawing, and later, of course, her fourth daughter, Princess Louise, later Duchess of Argyll, went in for sculpture, and executed the statue of her mother which is in the gardens outside Kensington Palace.

In 1855 the two elder children, Princess Victoria and the Prince of Wales, contributed some drawings they had done, to the Patriotic Fund Bazaar. These were extremely good, for art ran in this family, a trait inherited from their father. The drawings attracted the benevolent attention of critics, for they showed promise. In the end they were sold for the good cause. Princess Victoria's drawings fetched two hundred and forty pounds, quite a large sum for those days when money meant much more than it does today, and the young Prince's contribution brought in fifty-five guineas. Against keen competition they had done remarkably well.

3

Links with Germany

From his earliest days the Prince of Wales had always found his father far easier to get on with than his mother could ever be. It was always Prince Albert to whom the boy turned, realizing that he was far less narrow in outlook and had a sympathetically understanding nature. Nobody could have said that of the Queen. As a young girl she really had not had a chance, and was brought up entirely wrongly; it is a miracle that she did what she did when she came to the throne.

From the first the Prince found that his father could be relied upon to listen to him, and could sum up the 'ifs' and the 'buts' in a way his mother never did. She readily jumped to the wrong conclusions, but his father would always establish a situation, and make it easy for the lad to understand what he meant. His mother had a feminine tendency to lay down the law, and, of course, he was too young to see that this is a familiar habit with the fair sex. For generations they had played second fiddle in life's orchestra, and especially at that particular time in the history of England it was easier for a man to wield power than for a woman.

Victoria had reigned as Queen for several months before she had ever met her husband, and she was well used to rapping out orders, which had to be obeyed to the minute. The whole household knew that.

Her eldest son did not realize for some years that the fact that his mother was Queen had changed her so very much. She had come to a difficult throne, at a period of time when it was growing slightly ragged, as she knew. She had had to be commanding, to free herself from the errors of judgment made by her predecessors; to do this, she *had* to command. Essentially she had become stern, because as a girl, she had had no commanding appearance, but was slight and had bright eyes and pretty hair. Also she had been a little shy, and who would not have been, living the dull life that she had lived in Kensington Palace all those years?

Later, with the help of her most brilliant husband, she managed to put things right, changing ragged, hungry (in places unpleasant) England to a more comfortable mode of living, and she had done admirably. She had divided the country into classes, the royals and the peerage, the professional classes, and the middle classes. There were better living conditions! Home became the place on which one could draw the curtains and shut out the rest of the world. She *had* done well.

Then, when she married, her husband managed to show her the bitter mistakes of her indifferent education and knowledge. She owed everything to him! He taught her to be Queen, and he made her great. When the Jubilee years came and everyone (including myself) had a mug emblazoned with "Longest and most glorious reign, God bless her", it was the Prince Consort we owed everything to, for he was the man who had educated her. On the contrary, she and her son were poles apart.

He had inherited nothing of Victoria's narrow-mindedness. He found it hard to be serious for long, whilst she was a reserved woman and seldom saw a joke, and, when she did, did not laugh easily. She lost her girlishness very young, soon after her eldest son was born, for being a queen is a demanding job, and she was having children rapidly.

It was Prince Albert who persuaded her to take the children out with her, for the people loved seeing Bertie and the Princess Royal in their mother's carriage with her.

Once she had danced every night, but that had been a passing phase, no more. Now, with practically a baby arriving every year, she had become placid, mature, growing slightly stout, and to her horror *Punch* mentioned this!

So far as the eldest son's education was concerned, it was Prince Albert who set the pace. Bertie was clever, he had inherited his father's capacity for hard work, for Albert could beaver away at his desk all night if necessary, and even then appear bright and gay at breakfast.

The boy worked hard for the day when he would wear the crown, but the Queen confided in her husband that she thought he lacked the essential qualities of kingship. The Prince said that she was wrong, for he had the greatest faith in his heir.

It is strange how Victoria always felt this way about a son who was utterly charming, and had a brilliant brain, far more than she had – but that, of course, could have been the trouble.

It was in July, 1857 that Bertie, as mentioned, was taken to Germany to improve his German and to learn more about the country of his forbears. He stayed at Königswinter near Bonn on the Rhine. But he did admit that he never looked on Germany with the same love and light-hearted joy as he had always felt for France, and it is not surprising that he made an excursion there during his stay in Bonn. He owed so much to Paris, and that glorious first visit there, the sweetest memory of his life so far, so he said.

He had always hoped that one day a miracle would happen and that he would grow up and live in Paris.

"That is a pack of nonsense," his mother told him. "Your place is in this land where one day you will be the King."

Some people, not least Mr Gladstone, made a good deal of heavy weather over Bertie's kissing of that pretty charmer in Germany, but the visit was a great success and he seems there to have developed his lifelong passion for punning. He also visited the Austrian statesman Metternich, who was charmed by Bertie.

He was sixteen years old when his elder sister, the Princess Royal, became engaged to the Crown Prince Frederick William (Fritz) of Prussia , who was staying with them on one of those exquisite holidays at Balmoral, the creation of Prince Albert. The Princess was the most charming girl, very pretty and with her father's intellect. Fritz and she had walked on the heather-covered hills of Balmoral, where he had found some white heather, said to bring good fortune. This was when he first kissed her! He was little more than a boy himself, just nineteen, the son of stern parents, and it was then that he asked her to marry him when they were old enough, and she promised that she would.

They walked home hand-in-hand to tell Mama!

Although they were so very young, they were most deeply in love, and the Queen realized this. They had met originally as toddlers, playing in the Windsor nurseries together. Prince Albert and the Queen were anxious, for the girl was not even confirmed yet, but they realized that undoubtedly they were devoted to each other. Pussy did not want to live away from dear England which, of course, as Crown Prince he would have to do. He loved Britain, which he said had always received him with open arms.

He did not, admit then that he was privately terrified of his beloved's very commanding father and mother, though he found the home life of Balmoral utterly charming, and he could do more or less as he liked. He had been brought up against a severe background; later the Queen said that his spirit had been broken as a child, but at this time this defect did not show.

For the moment the engagement must be kept a secret. There would be time to discuss it in the spring when the bride-to-be had been confirmed and the thought of her marriage would be more acceptable.

In the bosom of her family, the eldest daughter had always been known as "Papa's pet", and none of them could think of the home without her.

She was confirmed that spring, and later her engagement to Fritz was announced. She was then seventeen. She was radiantly happy at the thought, and even more deeply in love. Her fiancé, too. It is so sad that her happiness faded, and ultimately her life sank into one almost of despair, for everything went wrong for her. The German in-laws disliked her, and did nothing to help her, and quite a lot to make matters worse. She was such a charming young girl, with the sweetest nature of all the Queen's children, a certain newspaper said, and when one thinks of the life that lay ahead of her, one is horrified that nothing could be done to help her.

When her wedding day came – on 25th January 1858 – it was one of those great occasions which the English people always enjoy so much and crowd out to see. Flags flew all over London, and crowds collected in the streets along the route. It was quite a long time since England had had a celebration of this nature, so that the people rather lost their heads in their determination to enjoy themselves, and to make the most of it.

Everyone was sure that this was no 'made marriage', as so many royal alliances had to be, for the story of how the young couple had fallen in love at Balmoral had got out, and everybody knew about it. The German family had been rather haughty about the marriage ceremony at St James's Palace; austere and offhand, and the Queen of England had been very angry with them, but what a predicament it was, for she dare not say too much lest it reflected on her young and most beloved daughter.

Princess Victoria was extremely young, of course, and so was he! She looked radiant as she entered the Chapel Royal wearing the most exquisite wreath of orange blossom, such as her mother had worn before her. Until her mother's marriage all the royal brides wore diamond tiaras, but Queen Victoria (with her strong German leanings) had brought in the vogue of orange blossom, and the country had taken to it in a very big way indeed. The sweet-smelling flower is associated with happiness, and most certainly Victoria's own marriage had been intensely happy.

The little bride of seventeen looked even younger, and the thought of parting with her devoted family and going to a new country for ever was the horror that kept on haunting her. On the night before the wedding she had told Mama that it worried her.

"How can I leave darling Baby?" she asked. This was the

Queen's youngest child, the little Princess Beatrice, not yet able to speak.

It was her kind father who told her that she was walking into a new life with the man whom she loved, and this would make all the difference in the world! Germany was a kind country, very much like England. Of course she would be happy with the man she loved.

Actually, when the moment to part came, the poor young girl broke down and wept bitterly. They tried to comfort her, but she clung to her father, to whom she was deeply attached. In the end, in a brave attempt to console her, he drove with the couple to Gravesend, where the royal yacht *Victoria and Albert* was waiting to receive the bride and groom, and take them across to her new country.

"What a dreadful moment!" exclaimed the Queen as the yacht sailed away.

Tremendous crowds had turned out to cheer them, as they drove off, but now it seemed that something had happened to the poor little bride, who was most desperately distressed over leaving her beloved home and especially her baby sister, who had shrieked to come with her, holding out her arms. It had all been very distressing, and she could not control her feelings. It was, so she told her father, almost as if some uncanny warning had come to her, that she was making a very grave mistake, and that she would never be happy again! It was a shocking thing to happen on her wedding day, and he tried to cheer her up, but, much as she loved the man whom she had married, nothing could stem her feelings of apprehension now.

This worried her father considerably, for Pussy's outburst had been so entirely unexpected. The young people were very much in love, and suddenly to find the little bride weeping her heart out was quite extraordinary, for she was not the type of girl who behaved like that. He said so. It was not that she felt that her marriage would be unhappy, for they had been devoted to each other, ever since that memorable day at Balmoral when they had come home hand in hand, she carrying the white heather they had found "for luck".

What on earth could be the trouble? Her father, asking himself this question, was far more upset than he cared to admit.

The girl had no idea what it was, save that quite suddenly she had had a premonition that she would be desperately unhappy, and she did not think that she could bear it. Her young husband and her kind father did their best to comfort her as they drove down to the quay. When the moment came for the final goodbye, she clung to the Prince Consort weeping bitterly. It was a farewell that he never forgot, for she was his favourite child and always would be. Driving back to the palace, he turned the incident over in his mind, and could not think what had happened, except that there *is* something in the superstitious side of life, and he only hoped that the marriage would turn out to be happy and a success. But now, for the first time, he had some horrible doubt about it. Had he done the right thing in letting her go? What else could he have done?

The royal parents had a miserable drive back home. Albert could hardly speak; in the end he decided to tell the Queen everything when she asked about it.

"At the last moment," he said, "she did seem to cheer up more, and she kissed me most affectionately, but it *was* so dreadful seeing her crying on her wedding day."

"She was devoted to her home, and to Baby," the Queen said.

Unfortunately, there was a good deal more behind that premonition than anybody thought at the time. The perceptive young girl found, when she arrived in Germany, that her adored husband was entirely over-ridden by his iron-willed family, and they were utterly demanding! He tried to console his princess, but the Kaiser was most stern, and the Kaiserin did nothing to help.

The Crown Prince went in awe of his parents and dare not stand up to them, as everybody knew, but they made it most unpleasant for the poor little bride from England. Vicky had so hoped that the new country would be home to her, and give her a second love, but it never tried to do this.

From the very outset of her marriage the Crown Prince suffered tremors of apprehension, which were heightened by her cold reception at the Prussian Court; while at home the Prince Consort could never forget her last plea to him – "Please, don't leave me!"

The Queen tried to cheer him. She said the thrill of her wedding day had been too much for Vicky, and when she got away with the man whom she loved, then everything would be all right! It had been a passing emotion, she insisted, and, although he said nothing, he still felt a strange anxiety for his favourite child.

He prayed that the girl would be happy in her new palace, though he admitted that home is where the heart is. Perhaps she had been a wee bit spoilt? Now she was married, and he consoled himself with memories of a glorious wedding day. By now, he thought, she would have set her fears at rest.

Fritz and Vicky had to face many trials in the early days. The Kaiser and Kaiserin had consented to the union, so they could not have disliked the thought too much, but a difficult, if not a tragic, life lay before Vicky, very different from those sunlit happy days at home. Here, in Prussia, she was contemptuously dubbed "the Englishwoman" by sycophants at the Court of the Hohenzollerns.

The palace which had been selected as the newly-married pair's quarters – the Old Schloss at Babelsberg – was pretentious and grand, but also old and draughty. All the windows rattled noisily in any wind; none of the doors fitted properly. The Crown Princess could not imagine how anyone had survived the discomforts and she also had to contend with rumours that the place was haunted. Nobody could ever imagine Queen Victoria abiding a window that rattled. She was most strict about keeping up the home properly and the young girl had thought that all mothers were the same. When she appealed to her mother-in-law, nothing was promised, and most certainly nothing was done! She was criticized by the Prussian Royal Family when she flung open the windows to air the place.

The girl kept thinking of the "Whyte Lady" whom someone had spoken of with awe, and she was constantly terrified that she herself would 'see something'. But there she was, in a draughty, door-banging palace, and there was nothing she could do about it!

She suffered from bad colds, which she had never had at home and which distressed her very much. All of a sudden, it seemed that this royal marriage for love had gone sour on them.

The Queen, used to comfort in her own family homes – in London, Windsor and Balmoral – found it very difficult to understand her eldest daughter's pathetic letters from Germany; she and her husband thought at first that it was a bad attack of homesickness. In the end Bertie was sent to visit her, preceded by his parents' advice to his sister to try to bring out his better qualities, as according to his father he was 'a cunning lazybones'.

Bertie was shocked at the conditions under which Vicky was living; the draughty, door-banging, window-rattling palace, and the story of a ghost! The little princess was now pregnant, and he thought that all this was extremely bad for her, and the in-laws should realize it! But the in-laws were indifferent, to say the least, and Fritz weakly submitted to their will.

Naturally Queen Victoria was very anxious for her own very young child, the more so in view of the way the German in-laws had behaved up to date, and she declared she would never entirely trust them again. She was so devoted to dear Pussy, and she very much wanted to be with her when her first grandchild was born.

Unfortunately, she had a heavy list of engagements, which she could not possibly break, and she wrote to the Kaiser and said that she was anxious for Vicky. She wanted to send over an English obstetrician to be with the child at the time. They did not actually refuse, though they were hardly gracious about it, but the *accoucheur* was given the details of the Crown Princess's case and told that he could see her nearer the time, as her German doctors were quite capable of handling affairs.

When the birth began the English doctor was only allowed to stand in the far corner of the room, never to come anywhere near the young Princess. But the German doctors made the most shocking muddle of it, as it turned out to be an unexpectedly difficult birth, for the child lay badly. The English doctor had warned the Germans of this when he had first examined the Princess, but they did not believe him.

So he had to wait until a German brought the son and heir into the world – on Mozart's birthday, 27th January. The baby's left shoulder was crushed under him. They tried to cover this mistake, and they said that later he could be operated on, but they could do nothing at the moment to bring his withered left arm to life. The English surgeon thought now was the only time for an operation, and he told the Queen so. The news distressed her.

The boy who came into the world that January day in 1859 ultimately became Kaiser Wilhelm II, and he went through life harassed by this disability, for which he always blamed his English mother. It was no fault of hers, and he should have blamed the German surgeons for not operating at the outset. The English surgeon would have done this, and he told the Queen that he did not think they would ever get the arm right now. It is possible that this warped his mind, and changed him, for he never liked his mother. As the surgeon from England said, the damage increased and his arm was practically useless, whereas, if the fault had been corrected immediately after birth it could have been put, not absolutely right, but made infinitely better than it was. Despite the churlish attitude to his mother which developed in later years, for some extraordinary reason, Willy became the old Queen's favourite grandson, perhaps because he was the first.

4

In the New World

The Prince of Wales learned a good deal from his study visit to Königswinter. His knowledge of German improved – indeed, to the end of his days he spoke with a guttural accent – and he gained an insight into the German military character which, before and during his brief reign as King, no doubt strengthened his affection for France and the French way of life. But it was in Germany that he began also to exhibit symptoms of what Victorian England regarded as a failing – a deep attraction for beautiful women. The 'kissing incident' was an early example of this, and thereafter Bertie found the pursuit of love interesting and even inspiring.

Of course, he did not get much time for amorous adventures, as his tutors – with an apprehensive eye on the Queen, who expected her son to work and nothing else – kept him in the same educational straitjacket, from which he occasionally was released for walking tours, although even then his father expected him to write home at length about his detailed impressions of Germany and its people. Prince Albert was not satisfied with 'mere bare facts'. Certainly it was no holiday. Nobody seems to have given the boy a holiday up to then, for this was not the mode of the day – and there was so much for a future King to absorb.

In those days holidays were not the thing to have. One could not work a young person hard enough, especially one born to high estate. Victoria, with her lack of a proper education, was certainly determined to see that her son had one. None must spare the boy. [It is not without interest to record that the future Emperor Wilhelm II, his nephew and Victoria's favourite grandson, was to undergo possibly an even more strenuous and rigid discipline at the hands of his German tutors.]

Albert Edward had a quick brain, but he found study a bore. He was assuredly no bookworm, and when he grew up he preferred reading newspapers to books. His handsome bearing constantly reminded his mother of her Hanoverian 'wicked uncles' – and she had too many unpleasant memories of George IV at Brighthelmstone with the Catholic Mrs Fitzherbert, the uncrowned Queen of England.

When he returned from Germany after his study tour the Prince of Wales was given an allowance and admonished by his mother to control his tastes and fancies and not to wear anything extravagant or 'slang'. He earnestly wished to join the Army – as had his predecessor, George IV, as a young man; but all the Queen offered him was an opportunity to pass a military examination when the occasion arose (which meant when she decreed it). The Heir to the Throne must be above armies – and navies, for that matter – as he must be above all political parties.

It was at this time when he came home from Germany that he found his mother more worried than he had ever known her to be before.

She was anxious about her youngest son, Prince Leopold, later Duke of Albany. He was the most difficult of all her children, infected with haemophilia, a blood disease, which meant that, with the slightest scratch, he *could* quite easily bleed to death.

Kind Mrs Lily had also been anxious for him; when he was born she drew the doctor's attention to some small symptoms, which she said that she did not like! She might be untrained, but the good midwife was extremely clever with babies. At first the doctors had glossed over her concern for the babe, and had held back the truth, but, in the end, the Queen had to be told what had happened. The new baby was a haemophiliac.

If he had a fall, or a cut (so that he bled), he could die: he would have to be protected and guarded carefully all his life.

The poor Queen had been most dreadfully distressed over this, so much so that she insisted that the doctors told her the full details, keeping nothing from her. She always wanted all the facts, however heartbreaking. The doctors had to admit that this troublesome disease was handed on through the *women* of the family (the one thing that they did not wish to tell her). It was a disease that a woman never developed, but a woman *could* hand it on to her sons.

There was nothing one could do to prevent it, or to cure it. The Queen must have been shattered by this, for it had come through *her*. The strange thing was that she had had seven children before this hereditary disease showed itself. The first seven were absolutely all right, but she had to be warned that this trouble *could* recur through her daughters.

It was indeed carried on by her favourite and youngest daughter, Princess Beatrice, whose only daughter became Queen Victoria Eugenie (Ena) of Spain when she married the young King Alfonso XIII. Both Queen Ena's eldest and youngest sons had this. If the old Queen had lived long enough to know it, she would have been horrified, for she adored Princess Beatrice, and had always predicted that her "little girl" would marry a king.

As Victoria's children grew up life was no easier for her. Her darling eldest child, "dear little Vicky", was happily married to the German Crown Prince, but was made wretched by her in-laws. Vicky's eldest son, the heir, was never able to use his twisted arm properly.

As he matured the Prince of Wales became extremely worried for his sister in Germany, for they had meant a lot to one another in nursery days. His visits to her both when he was studying in Germany and later appalled him: she hardly ever saw a friend, and he *did* write to his mother about it. But there was nothing that anyone could do!

"He is not the same as his sister, Your Majesty," Mrs Lily had said, when she scooped him up into her arms, for the first time. "They will never be really alike, but he *is* going to be a great king!" She was accurate there!

The problem of the Prince's future education was now very much in mind. He was confirmed in April 1858.

There had been much discussion about the selection of a house where he could live, until such time as he married, for, of course, he would *have* to wed eventually. He felt that Marlborough House, which was a possibility, was too close to Mama, and there, perhaps, he was wise! He was in a sense relieved when it was decided to send him and his tutors to the Surrey mansion, White Lodge, which stands in Richmond Park, and has superb views. This lovely house has set a roof over the head of many of our princes, and this was the one chosen for this young man.

It stands in the most romantic position, with a long clear road (leading from the one that goes to Roehampton Gate), to the house itself. It was built at a period when design was at its best.

His establishment in this new home would mean that, for the first time, he would be stepping out into the world. He longed for liberty. He was getting tired of parents for ever guiding him, and he knew that he was growing up. His mother had always been too ready to find fault, and he was out-growing her constant commands. His father was still kind and helpful, very considerate of his personal feelings, but it would be good to cut himself free, and have a real home where he could do more or less as he wished.

Nevertheless his father made it quite clear that at White Lodge the Prince would be "kept away from the world" for a few months. This would help to round off his education – under his tutors, Mr Gibbs and Mr Tarver – and also to ensure that he put in some study of military affairs. Eventually he was gazetted a lieutenant-colonel without any examination, a decision that he did not exactly like, but it was imposed on him – he really wanted to work his way up through the ranks.

He was also furnished with three equerries, two of them valiant soldiers (both winners of the Victoria Cross) and the third a young peer. Their orders from the Prince Consort were to make Bertie "the first gentleman in the country".

They were given detailed instructions about his appearance, deportment and dress, his manners, and how he should amuse himself provided his amusements also helped to develop his mind. Naturally the boy was bored beyond measure at Richmond.

A welcome break came, however, with the visit to his sister in Berlin when she was expecting the birth of the future Wilhelm II. After that he went on to Rome to study archaeology, art and current affairs. He was also told that afterwards he would be sent to the universities at Oxford and then Cambridge, and during the vacations there he would be able to get in some military training and undertake tours abroad.

Again in Rome he had to send his father detailed accounts of his experiences, but the Prince Consort was not pleased with his letters, and the Queen, of course, compared them unfavourably with those which she regularly received from the Princess Royal in Berlin.

On his way home by sea he enjoyed "plenty of larking" in Gibraltar. After a cruise along the Spanish coast he spent a few days in Lisbon visiting his cousin, King Pedro V.

When he returned he was sent to Christ Church, Oxford, but was not allowed to live the life of an ordinary undergraduate. Six other undergraduates were chosen to be his companions, and he was lectured daily by specially chosen professors.

It was at Oxford that he began to put on weight, as he employed a chef of his own, and this chef was an expert in rich and sometimes indigestible dishes. Prince Albert warned his son against putting an undue strain upon his liver, and expressed his view that Bertie was "a thorough and cunning lazybones". Yet the young Prince did well enough in his terminal examinations, much to his mother's surprise.

During another visit to his German relations he called on his father's old adviser, Baron Stockmar, in Coburg. Then came his first big adventure. He was sent to tour Canada and the United States of America.

His father felt that this experience would be a tremendous help to him later on. It was the sort of exacting tour that only a very young man in strong health could possibly undertake, and later it would be a splendid thing to have done.

First-hand knowledge of Canada, and the States, would be of the greatest help to him, and travel, as wide as this, was something few previous princes had ever done.

He, for his own part, wanted to enjoy life, and I think that, all things considered, he achieved this end, though most certainly he did work very hard to get it. He was now a very merry young man, only too anxious to taste of the good things of life. He wrote regularly to his elder sister in Germany, sympathized with her many troubles, and wished that he could help her, for life was working out extremely badly for her. The poor girl was unpopular, for no fault of her own, but simply because her in-laws were so objectionable.

Her brother told her of the prospective journey to North America, and how thrilled he was at the thought of this.

He completed his time at Oxford with none too many crises, probably because he was feeling his way, and then went off on this amazing tour.

Privately he was a little alarmed to be with strangers, with no Papa to turn to if things became complicated. He was destined to be one of those princes who, all his life, *did* find things becoming complicated.

The idea was that, when he came to the throne, he would be the first monarch properly prepared to accept the tremendous burdens demanded of him. He was eighteen years old when he left Plymouth – good-looking, and very strong! He would need every ounce of strength that he had got, to go off alone with his gentlemen to see the other side of the Western world and learn from it.

In his later years, the Prince said, "That was when I first learnt what it was like to feel *really* tired! I'd only played at it before I set out to see the other side of the world." And he laughed.

He admitted that it had demanded almost too great an effort, and that the strain was ghastly at moments, but it *had* taught him, as his father had predicted, more than anything else in his life! He got sick of the noise of the train and being for ever off to some new place, meeting strangers all the time, in a way that he had never done before. Wherever he went he got the most tremendous reception.

His father's very clever advice had been, "Don't think of yourself, think only of how other people want to see you, and be nice to them."

He stuck by that advice.

The young man adored his time in Canada, which came first, because his parents felt it was a quieter part of the world, and would get him used to the thrill and excitement which lay ahead for him in the United States. And, of course, it was a political courtesy to visit the British Dominion first.

He liked the life there, and the kindly, friendly people. He met Blondin, the French acrobat, and watched him walking along a tight-rope across Niagara Falls, pushing a man in a wheelbarrow. When Blondin got to the far side, the Prince, who had been watching closely all the time, said, "Well, thank God that's over!" Blondin offered to wheel the Prince back to the American side.

That *would* shake the entire world. What the Queen and the Prince Consort would have said to it, Heaven only knew! The idea was stopped very quickly, I imagine much to the poor young Prince's regret, and Blondin returned alone – on stilts – to the other side.

Bertie, as I have said, tired of the throb of the eternal trains, and would have done anything to get away from the sound of it. If he stayed in a town, the noise seemed to continue in his head when at last he got to bed. He remembered that his mother had warned him of this, and of the probability of feeling extreme exhaustion, but somehow he had never thought that it would affect himself.

He loved Canada. Whilst there his engagements were fairly serene, but it was different in the United States. What he did not realize was that time was creeping up on him, and the Americans as a nation found it difficult to take things calmly. He might have started on this tour as a boy, but he ended up as a man.

He was travelling as Baron Renfrew, though all the world and its wife knew this to be a pseudonym. Canada had abided by the ruling from the palace in England, but America was not the sort of country to be put off so easily.

The Americans were thrilled by the thought of entertaining the Prince, and he had been told that although official welcomes would be held, at no time would he be anyone but Baron Renfrew when he visited a town, made a speech or two, and then went on elsewhere.

"Not at all!" said the wildly enthusiastic Americans. "This is the Prince of Wales, and the Prince of Wales he is going to be whilst he is with us!"

They arranged enormous official receptions, perhaps the biggest the poor boy had ever seen, and the United States of America sets out to do this sort of thing extremely well. They had referred back to England to ask if the Prince could be the man he was, and not just an ordinary baron, which would give them infinitely more pleasure, if possible, whilst the charming and amiable young Prince was visiting them, but had received back the usual haughty message saying 'No'. He was travelling as Baron Renfrew. His mother was adamant over this and was accustomed to having her wishes obeyed. In real fact the Baron died the moment that the Prince entered the United States, for that country simply *would* not have it!

He was in Hamilton, Ontario, when all this argument was going on between Washington and Buckingham Palace, and he had no idea what lay ahead of him.

He had been told that big official welcomes were 'out', (he

was far too young to cope with that sort of thing); he was merely Baron Renfrew, who was to make the occasional speech, and nothing more.

But the wildly enthusiastic Americans had never had the Heir to the Throne visiting them before.

When he arrived at the border 30,000 Americans gave him the noisiest welcome the boy had ever heard. Moreover, the assembled bands of music made sure that the last had been heard of Baron Renfrew by striking up *God bless the Prince of Wales.*

"A bit hard on Mama!" he told his sister later, "but what could she do about it?"

When he got back home, worn out, weeks later, he said, "They would not take anything else," and laughed about it. "This is not what Mama wanted," he told the others with him. They knew that, and also that they would get into trouble for not having stopped it, but what could they do?

He was a very glowing young man, a trifle short, perhaps, but in those days men seemed shorter than they are today. The Prince found the contrast with polite Canada amusing. Masses of people rushed forward to shake his hand as he travelled from place to place in the special train, containing a luxury suite, placed at his disposal by the hospitable American Government.

The American newspapers had a field day wherever he went, and treated the public to the most sensational revelations. In particular they poked fun at the Prince's stately entourage, headed by the Duke of Newcastle, the Colonial Secretary; Lord St Germans, a Household official; General Bruce, his 'governor'; and other Court dignitaries, whose sedate English ways provoked the brash Americans to ribaldry.

But the Prince could do no wrong. He was wildly acclaimed, even by Irish Americans who could be regarded as being among the more anti-British elements of American society. Newcastle told the Queen that this was all a great practical education for Bertie and that "the development of mind and habit of thought is very perceptible".

"This is going to be a bit too exciting," the Prince said to one of his gentlemen at the beginning of the American tour.

There was one moment on the first day when his carriage, trying to get through to his hotel, came to a dead stop in a milling throng. The Prince was not in the least worried. He knew that his mother would be, but as he said in one of those carelessly gay moments of his, "She ought to have realized that this part of the world is *not* England and can't be expected to do what she tells it to do!"

Neither of his parents had anticipated such unbridled enthusiasm. And now every band in America was crashing out the 'forbidden' anthem – *God Bless the Prince of Wales*!

The Prince was horrified by the way the crowd were literally beaten back by the police to let his carriage through. Eventually he got safely to his hotel, and as he entered his suite and the strains of the Prince's anthem filled the air he remarked to one of his aides:

"God *help* the Prince of Wales is what they really mean!"

That was the day when he tasted his first mint julep. Privately he did not think much of it, but not for the world would he have admitted it.

He was easy to get on with, which is more than could be said for some of those who were with him, for they panicked over all the fuss, perhaps understandably, knowing that the Queen would never understand that her decrees were being disobeyed. But the Americans had decided that this good-looking boy with the blue eyes and the merry smile was going to be the most successful guest they had ever had.

As the triumphal tour progressed the Prince and his company began to feel the strain. Chicago, loud and brassy, impressed Bertie by its size: it was quite different from any of the towns he had visited in Britain, or France, or Germany. They certainly did things on a big scale here!

America was growing fast. In one village he visited near Chicago to do a little shooting he discovered that in five years the price of land had rocketed from just under a dollar to a hundred dollars an acre.

In his train, as it rolled into and out of St Louis, Cincinnati, Pittsburgh and Baltimore, the Prince was amazed at the great goodwill which gushed up from the ever-growing crowds. He must have reflected wryly that these were the descendants of Americans who, not many decades earlier, would have jeered his great-grandfather, King George III, through the streets had he ever visited his 'colonies'!

But it was all very tiring. The Duke of Newcastle had express instructions from Buckingham Palace which he found it utterly impossible to obey. The Queen had set forth a list of rules as to what the Prince could and – more important – could *not* do; but things were not working out according to plan. And how could one avoid it? The Prince must not be permitted to get overtired at any time.

Yet everything had been arranged beforehand – and the Americans had laid on a massive programme for their most thrilling and enchanting visitor.

The Prince wrote to tell his mother that far too great demands were being made on him. He had never known such tiredness. It was one series of State rides, visits to special places, dances at night: far too much had been fitted into the programme. He had had no idea that they could overdo it like this. The Duke of Newcastle came to the conclusion that the Americans were completely tireless! Far too many people wanted to see the Prince. Reception succeeded reception. No wonder the boy was overtired.

"The Americans ask too much," said Newcastle. "The Prince gets tired, and they won't take 'no' for an answer."

He was there to protect the Prince of Wales as much as he could, and get him safely back again when the tour ended. He knew that Her Majesty would be definitely displeased if he did not carry out the programme properly, and he saw one of her dreaded 'talkings-to' ahead of him, but what could he do?

The Prince, although a very strong young man, was showing some signs of distress. King Leopold had written to him from Belgium saying what a wonderful success the tour was, and that this trip should teach him a great deal that princes had to know.

The boy read the letter. "Too much!" he said. "This trip has taught me that you *can* be worked to death!"

He made one of the most brilliant speeches, written for him, of course, and afterwards one member of the eager audience rushed at him, clasped his hand, and said. "Begad, Sire, come back in four years' time, and stand for the Presidency!"

He laughed about that, and said it was the most eager response from the crowd that he had ever known. He was quite informal with people, always smiling and this made him tremendously popular.

He laughed a lot, too, for he had already found that laughter had a special appeal of its own, and he laughed whenever he could, but, as he wrote to his mother, it was very, very hard work, for, of course, they expected everything of him.

Although his own party still most loyally insisted on speaking of the Prince as 'Baron Renfrew', nobody else copied them. They sang "God bless the Prince of Wales" with gusto, and souvenirs were being sold in the streets with his face on them and the three white feathers of his badge on the other side.

Wonderful balls were given in his honour; he was at the age which adores dancing, and he danced extremely well. But, as he said, you could have too much of a good thing! Some of the banquets were so magnificent that he could not believe that they were true. Yet at other times he was quite shocked, because there were dancers at the balls who did not even wear evening dress (at that period essential in England), and twice he saw men who kept their hats on! He said to one of his suite: "I must say that after this visit to America nothing will ever surprise me again."

Then he asked: "Don't they realize that the right dress is important?"

"They don't seem to think so, Sir," was the reply, "and it appears to be permitted, for nobody tries to stop them."

5

One Continual Triumph

Pittsburgh vied with all the other cities to do him proud. The train was met and he was escorted to his hotel – for the most part he stayed in hotels – with a band playing the strangest music which he at first failed to recognize as the National Anthem and, when he was told, he merely wondered what Mama would have said! He was enjoying the fun, but had to admit that he had never felt so tired before. His right arm ached from eternal saluting and handshaking – "pressing the flesh", as the Americans now call it – and he thought it would never be the same again.

In Washington he went to stay at the White House, where President James Buchanan, a benign elderly gentleman, recalled that he had last seen the Prince when he was a child at Buckingham Palace.

The President's hostess was his niece, Miss Harriet Lane. In a letter to the Queen the Prince described her as "a particularly nice person, and very pretty".

Among presents which the Prince had been asked to deliver to the President were two large Winterhalter portraits of the Queen and the Prince Consort.

A voyage up the Potomac to George Washington's house at Mount Vernon was, of course, an indispensable part of American protocol. While there the Prince planted a chestnut sapling near the grave of his great-grandfather's great enemy. (The tree died a few years later, and the Prince sent a replacement).

On to Philadelphia, the "City of Brotherly Love", where he visited a new prison and saw ex-Judge Vandersmith, who had

Queen Victoria in 1854 with Edward Prince of Wales, the Princess
Royal, Prince Alfred and Princess Alice (a Fenton photograph
of 1854)

The Prince of Wales with his tutor Mr Gibbs

been convicted on corruption and forgery charges. "Talk away, Prince!" said the judge when the Prince stopped at his cell for a chat. "There's plenty of time – I'm here for twenty years!"

But it was New York which of all the American centres he had visited left the most profound impression on the young Prince. The city had determined to outdo all the other cities and states put together.

By some miscalculation the Prince's train was several hours late arriving, so it was near sunset when he arrived, to be driven in a barouche down Broadway. The coach had been specially made for the occasion.

He was cheered all the way from the station, for despite the late arrival New York had mustered in strength to see 'Lord Renfrew'.

The fiction was still kept up, but everybody knew it was the Queen's eldest son and gave him 'the treatment'. He ached all over. He felt as though his right arm had been broken – "That is the way they are breaking me in," he said ruefully – and that nobody had taken the trouble to set it.

When his mother warned him what he was likely to encounter on a tour of this kind she had said, "It is the sort of thing you can do only when you are very young." He now came to the conclusion that she had known what she was talking about!

As he bowed from the balcony of his Fifth Avenue hotel in reply to the crowd's boisterous welcome he felt as though his neck had a crick in it. But he told his hosts that the accommodation they had provided for him was far more comfortable than his own rooms in Windsor Castle and Buckingham Palace.

But there was certainly one big difference. When he awoke at Buckingham Palace the birds were singing in the garden, but in New York he was awakened by some dreadful brass band playing the interminable *God Bless the Prince of Wales* under his window. He was sick to death of being the Prince of Wales, and told his valet so.

For the first time he realized what the Queen had to put up with when she went on tour, yet she never seemed to flag. He wondered how she did it.

As yet the tour had passed without any really unpleasant scene, but this did happen in New York one day as he left his hotel to go to his waiting carriage and make a grand sight-seeing tour.

The street was jammed with people, and then he saw a rather odd-looking man pushing his way towards him, and shaking his fist violently. How he had got so close nobody would ever know.

He got far *too* close, and then called out, "You will never be the King of England, because the time for kings is past!"

Then the guards got him. The Prince was not alarmed, but extremely worried because he thought that the crowd was antagonistic and might lynch the man. He called to them: "Don't hurt him! Be good to him!" in a commandingly loud English voice which could be heard above the hubbub. To his own suite he said: "I only pray that nothing like this happens again, and I do pray that they behave decently to the poor fellow."

It turned out that he was not an American at all, but an English sailor who had what is known as 'a bee in his bonnet' about the Royal Family, saying that all of them were overpaid for doing nothing! That made the Prince laugh when he heard the explanation.

"That just shows how little he knows about it! He had better come here and take on two days of my tour, and that would teach him what it's like!"

He would not have admitted it to the Americans but he had now come to the time when he was just longing to catch sight of the ship that would take him home! His mother would never know how much America asked of him, and what he had to do, but he would tell her all about it when he got back. He was beginning to wonder whether he would ever see the peace and quiet of England again.

A spectacular ball was finally given in his honour, and he

made the most enormous impression at it. He looked so young, so slim, and the orchestra struck up with the English National Anthem, and on the second he sprang to attention! They, of course, mouched about, and even talked, but the young man in whose honour the ball was given lifted his hand to salute his mother as the National Anthem ended.

They were greatly impressed.

The Mayor, Fernando Wood, presented him with a gift from an old lady who was ill and could not be present at the ball as she had hoped. It was a pair of gloves that she had made for him, far too big, but he wore them, for this was part of his training.

"A Prince to be proud of," was the general verdict.

But, of course, it had been noticed that he had an eye for a pretty girl, and New York produced their loveliest for him. He was never slow to look back at them, for he was something of a connoisseur of pretty women.

The ball was held at the Academy of Music. Three thousand of the cream of New York society had been invited, but the place was besieged by another two thousand who thought they should have been invited too.

The organizers failed to control this vast crowd, the barriers were crashed down as the uninvited guests stormed in – and just before the Prince arrived the floor caved in.

Luckily nobody was hurt. A huge gang of carpenters carried out emergency repairs while the guests had supper.

To the young Prince anything like this was rather a good joke, and, as nobody was hurt, he was quite happy. He had received the most wonderful welcome of his life in New York, and he sat down with the other guests to the best supper that he had ever eaten.

After two hours the floor was ready for dancing, and back to the ballroom they went.

Possibly in their haste to get through the job quickly, the workmen had not been too painstaking for there came some of the most extraordinary sounds from under the floor, and ultimately it was discovered that one of the carpenters had got himself trapped under the boards. He was uninjured; in fact, he was rather the hero of the hour, as the Prince congratulated him when they got him out!

Bertie enjoyed this party very much, though he could have wished that they had provided him with more pretty young partners. As it was, he was almost monopolized by their mothers!

The world was far bigger than he had ever thought, and far more encouraging than he had expected it to be. Nobody criticized him, whereas in England a day seldom passed when some newspaper did not make some rude remarks about him, and privately he got very sick of it. He was seeing the world as no other Prince of Wales had done before him, forming his own conclusions about it, and the people in it.

On the Sunday morning, in strict accordance with the instructions from England, he had to attend divine service at Holy Trinity Church. Mama had said that, whatever else her son did, *this* was most necessary.

His hosts had warned him of it, and the right preparations had been made, to receive him there at the correct hour, eleven in the morning. He would be met by the English bishop. The news of this got out, and a lot of people (most of whom had never been inside a church before) saw this as the best possible means of seeing the young man, and for quite a long time having a first-class view of him. The Prince had already discovered that, if the Americans wished to see someone, they would stop at nothing to do so! He wanted to go to church quietly, as he always did at home.

"America is not quite like England," he was told by the bishop, who was taking the service.

He was right! He was not at all sure if this service had guests with tickets, or if anyone could come! If the latter, he was already sorry for himself. But this was a duty that could not be overlooked, and Mama would be doing exactly the same thing in London, the family with her. He rather wished that he could have been with them.

Now, knowing how pushful the Americans could be, he did

ask that suitable arrangements could be made, for he was under constant strain. He was quite right in being suspicious that in the United States, anything could happen, and probably would.

Admission to the church was by ticket only, and these – as in the case of the ball – had been allotted to the chosen. But crowds more had got there by nine in the morning, two hours before the service was due to start.

Everyone had gone to see what they could of the young Prince. Inside the church, in the pew where the Prince would sit, there was a pair of the most magnificent prayer books, bound in red morocco leather, and, on the covers, the three white feathers, which was the badge of the Prince of Wales. The books were said to have cost two hundred and fifty dollars; they were an anonymous gift to the church for his use.

When he arrived he received the most tremendous reception. The church, already crammed to overflowing, rose to greet him. People even stood on the pew seats to get a better view, but those behind them saw nothing and a row started. It was not the entry to which a Prince is accustomed, for in England things went quietly, and people did what they were told. People had to be quietened down!

"Remember that we are in the House of the Lord," an English verger reminded them.

The Prince himself entered, demure and handsome, faithful to what he believed to be his duty. He walked up the aisle to his place, apparently noticing nothing of the heads poked forward to catch sight of him. At least he knew how to behave.

His visit to the New World was the most exhausting expedition he had ever undertaken. The doctors warned him to take care not to overdo things; they had been so right! He had never felt so fatigued, but he insisted that the Queen was not told of this, for she would make a supreme fuss, and blame everybody else for it, when it was all part of the job, and he knew it.

He accepted mistakes, unlike his Mama, for this young man

was placidly amiable, more so than either his father or mother. He enjoyed seeing places and meeting people. His reception in New York surprised even his 'governor', General Bruce, who wrote that "the affair has been one continual triumph". The Prince had undergone "no slight trial" and his patience, temper and good breeding had been "severely taxed."

Undoubtedly he had done a lot of good for the monarchy by coming here. His visit had steadied the relationship between England and the United States. Americans adored the good-looking young boy, who was so gay and friendly, and his presence had strengthened the bonds between them.

They suggested that he had a few days off, holidaying with no commitments, halfway through.

"I really do need it," he admitted.

The Queen hoped he had not made himself ill, but his father was enchanted by the reports of his good work. The Prince himself felt that the time had come when he could no longer be nervous, and the extreme warmth of the American welcome helped him enormously. He could laugh himself round a difficult corner!

"It is quite magical what you can do if only you can make people laugh," he told an equerry.

Mugs were given away to children, with his picture on them, and wherever these mugs were the Union Jack was flying gaily, and crowds were waiting to see him.

"It is all very well for *them*," he said, very tiredly indeed, after one big show which had completely exhausted him. "*They* don't have to do it all over again tomorrow!"

He felt sometimes that perhaps he was shown only what his hosts intended him to see, yet he had spoken to thousands of people, and often he broke away and spoke to others who had not expected to get near him. It made him intensely popular. He had learnt a lot about them, and, even if he had not had the chance to study them closely, he did feel that he had done more than most.

He must have done amazingly well, because he became the

hero of the United States, and, anyway for the moment, he was the man for them. It was a land that had no kings of its own, but, as he said, "My goodness! *how* they love a crown!"

His mother and father had been right when they had said that a tour of this kind could only be undertaken when a man was very young, but it could easily be the corner-stone on which his entire career was built!

Yet the Queen was, he knew, still very critical of him, and only too ready to suggest that he was too familiar with nobodies, whilst his father praised him.

"He knows what he is doing, and he is doing *well*" insisted the Prince Consort.

The Queen reluctantly agreed that Bertie was bright at times and had done better than she expected in the United States. The news she received from people over there assured her of this.

At the same time she was intensely annoyed that they had actually 'banished' the Baron Renfrew, and had then struck up with that far too familiar tune "God Bless the Prince of Wales!"

Of course, Canada had been easier to manage, for the people there were not so wildly demonstrative, and there had not been this mad rush to entertain him. Also he had had some chance of relaxation, which he did not get in the United States.

He left America in October 1860. After a trip to Boston he had met everybody of importance (Longfellow, Oliver Wendell Holmes, and Emerson amongst them), and he had done everything that he had been told to do. He had loved most of it, in particular six thousand firemen giving a display which was so magnificent that it actually took his breath away.

Before he left he was taken to Bunker's Hill and then to Harvard, but he was rushed through these visits so that he could board H.M.S. *Hero* at Portland, Maine. This was not the age of luxury liners and the royal party were warned that the weather ahead was not very good. Large crowds had come to

see him off, but by now he was worn out and only too thankful
to be leaving for home, where at least he could go to bed and
get a rest.

The sea roughened.

There were moments when he felt most dreadfully ill, for he
was *not* a first-class sailor and the *Hero* was a small ship
lashing about in the fury of the storm. That must have been
something that he never forgot, and it came after a most
tremendous strain that he had endured with great courage.

When the Prince left – seen off by the Governor of Maine
and the Queen's Canadian Ministers – he had hoped to be
home in time to celebrate his nineteenth birthday, but the
voyage lasted twenty-six days.

There were moments when he felt that undoubtedly the
ship would be dashed to pieces: he had never been so sick
before, and there was little that could be done to help him.

There was much anxiety at home when the ship failed to
arrive, and two vessels were sent out from Plymouth to search
for it. At last, on 15th November, the *Hero* docked at Plymouth
and the Prince was driven without further ceremony to
Windsor, declaring: "Thank God for home!" The greatest joy
that the castle could offer him was the fact that it *did* stand
still. He was some time finding his feet.

His father was very pleased with him for what he had done.
It had been a goodwill tour, and had been the corner-stone of
a friendlier relationship between Britain and America, and he
was proud to have done so well.

Privately the Queen was not sure that she approved of
everything that had happened, though obviously the Prince
kept the liveliest bits to himself. But he did tell her that he had
been touched by the great kindness of complete strangers, and
that it had almost swept him off his feet.

He thought that the United States was a far gayer and more
independent country than his own, though Mama felt that he
should have made a stand and refused to let them call him 'the
Prince', when he knew perfectly well that he was supposed to
be Baron Renfrew as she had so carefully arranged! But he

replied that nothing in this world would stop the Americans from doing what they *wanted* to do: they just did it!

The Queen had received a most glowing letter from the President of the United States, telling her of the great success of her eldest son and how mad the States had gone about him! She told Bertie of the letter, but did not actually show it to him. She had always been the most extraordinary woman with this eldest son of hers, for she hardly thanked him, though he had made a marvellous tour, and, at his age, it was unbelievable.

"I don't want him to lose his head!" Victoria explained.

"I think one should give praise, where praise is due," his father told her. "He did far more than either you or I could have done at his age, and, because he was so young, he managed to get through without being too exhausted. Give honour where it is right!"

She said nothing.

Her husband must have wondered what he could do to make her more sympathetic with her son. He had never been able to understand her strange reserve towards the Heir to the Throne. Naturally the boy had come to the age when he noticed this, and her aloofness *did* worry his father very much; perhaps the boy knew it. At most times the Prince Consort could manage Queen Victoria, but now he began to wonder if, under it all, she was half jealous of her son? He had a charm that she had not, a welcoming, amiable virtue which the world recognized and liked.

The tour had matured Bertie. He had flung aside boyhood and had come out into the world. But it was rather difficult, after having worked so hard overseas, doing everything that was demanded of him, and then coming home to find Mama laying down the law and ordering him about.

She was for ever reproving him, why had he not done this or that, in that exacting manner of hers!

What he did not know was that even while he was battling with sea-sickness on the stormy return voyage across the Atlantic the Queen was writing to the Princess Royal in Berlin saying how immensely popular her brother was in North America and that he "really deserves the highest praise, which should be given him all the more as he was never spared any reproof".

The Prince was no doubt looking forward to a long holiday, but after only three days at Windsor he was hurried back to Oxford, where half the Christmas term was nearly over.

He found it hard getting back into the swim of undergraduate life. He therefore looked forward to spending the Christmas holidays at Windsor. Here he went riding in the Great Park, a part of his mother's kingdom which he loved.

Then came the Christmas festivities which the Queen and the Prince Consort celebrated in the German fashion, with roast turkey and beef, mince pies and a plum pudding with little charms mixed in with it – a ring which, if you got a slice with it, meant that you would wed in the New Year; a button for the bachelor or the old maid; a tiny horseshoe for luck; and a sixpenny piece for prosperity.

There was also a tiny china doll. If you got that in your slice of Christmas pudding it meant that you would give birth to a baby in the coming year.

The Prince of Wales got it – and laughed uproariously. But Mama did not think it in the least funny.

6

Romantic Phase

The Prince of Wales did feel very much better for his stay at Windsor, doing nothing for a change and being at nobody's beck and call.

With Oxford University behind him, he was due to leave for a spell at Trinity College, Cambridge, in mid-January. He rather looked forward to this new experience.

The North American tour had taught him a lot. He was far better informed now, and he felt that he would get a great deal more out of Cambridge than he would ever get out of Oxford. He had enjoyed his time at Christ Church, but felt that he had been too well guarded, as he told his father: he wished to mix much more with other undergraduates when he went to Cambridge, and not just with friends who had been selected for him by his elders and betters.

Although his father fully understood this argument, he pointed out that the heir to the throne could not expect to enjoy quite the same liberty as an ordinary undergraduate. His life was too precious!

Also it was so easy to get himself into scrapes which instantly became public and were seized on and exaggerated by the newspapers. The usual little sins that a young man committed at university became news if they were committed by the Heir to the Crown, and for that reason he simply *must* be more careful that other undergraduates.

Therefore, as at Oxford, the Prince of Wales was not allowed to live in college. At Cambridge he was quartered at Madingley Hall, four miles outside the city. From here the

Prince rode on horseback into college every morning, or drove there in a phaeton.

With the connivance and help of the sympathetic and understanding Master of Trinity, William Whewell, he was allowed to keep a set of rooms in college for his use on exceptional occasions, and that made life more tolerable for him.

Victoria liked the idea of the Cambridge experiment, but she was becoming more and more critical of her son. She was essentially old-fashioned, even for those days, but Bertie was a product of the new world, a very different one from the Victorian one, when the blinds were drawn on any misdemeanour and scandal was swept under the carpet.

Deep down in her heart I suspect that the Queen never forgot her first impression of Bertie as a newly-born infant in the kind arms of Mrs Lily, and it was then that she recognized a likeness to George IV, the man whom she detested most in all her life.

Yet there was no reason why they should grow up alike, because this was a far wiser young man than his Hanoverian predecessor had been; he had had the best training that he could have, and maybe he would become one of the greatest of kings.

The Queen lectured him just before he left for Cambridge on 18th January 1861. In the course of her remarks she accused him of something which he had not done, and he denied it. She said haughtily,

"Remember that I am your Queen!"

He flashed back: "You are my mother first!"

The Queen admitted later in private that this forthright reply quite dismayed her. When she thought it out – and she was one of those women who *did* think things out – she must have felt that she had gone rather farther than she should have done, but somehow she could not help it with this son.

His future was so important to his country, the country that she had made great. Her husband said that she argued with Bertie far too much and that, after his great tour, surely he had the right ideas?

Prince Albert also had a long and serious talk with the young Prince before he went off to Cambridge. He told his son that whatever happened, there must not be too much of what he called "the girl business". He knew that his son had now arrived at the age when beauty in a woman caught his eye! He liked talking to pretty girls, and they *did* capture his fancy very easily indeed!

At Cambridge he would come under the law and order of the university, and although he might think one could evade their rules and regulations, it never paid in the long run. He told his son that the splendid tour that he had just taken (and on which he had done so well) was nothing by which to compare the rest of the world. At Cambridge he would *not* be the leading figure. Even the Prince of Wales was treated more or less like everybody else, and he might be laying himself open to stern reproof, which every undergraduate expects and very often gets. He must forget that tour, and settle down to real hard work if he was to do anything and get anywhere.

"No man can get his own way *all* the time," his father told him, warningly but very kindly. "Even when you are the King you will have to remember that you still are the servant of the people and one of the most overworked servants in the State."

But the Prince was at an age when he was all out for a little fun. One was only young once, he told himself, and there was nothing he liked better than a first-class spree – or 'lark', as he called it.

Undoubtedly the North American tour had enabled him to spread his wings and had whetted his appetite for 'larks' – and he was going to the right place for them.

He certainly made many more friends at Cambridge than he had done at Oxford, and here can be seen the beginnings of his later attachment to the Rothschilds, for one of his fellow-undergraduates was Nathaniel ('Natty') Rothschild. The Prince also took a liking to Charles Kingsley, then Regius Professor of Modern History: he attended his lectures regularly and, because he was interested, benefited from them.

But the Prince chafed against the rules and regulations of

Cambridge. He had not abandoned his earlier ambition of an Army career, but General Bruce – who continued at Cambridge as his 'governor' – was not satisfied with him and complained to the Prince Consort about his "intolerance" and his disposition to form "hasty and mistaken judgements".

The General also felt that through his "love of excitement" the Prince tended to stray into the company of "the idle and the frivolous".

Bruce was a martinet, but under the eagle eye of the Queen he had to be careful. The Prince was by no means an easy young man to handle, and the General erred on the side of severity.

There was much talk in Court circles at this time of the necessity for the Prince of Wales to settle down in marriage with an acceptable princess, who would match up to his mother's requirements as well as his own.

But for the present his constant plea to join the Guards could no longer be ignored, and the Prince Consort, after a talk with Bruce at Cambridge, agreed that Bertie should during the summer vacation take a ten-week infantry training course with the Grenadiers at the Curragh camp near Dublin.

As Guards officers at that time had "a way with women" – and this was known to Bruce – he agreed that the Prince should be subjected to the strictest discipline while he learnt how to do every officer's job from ensign upwards.

But the plan devised was ridiculously ambitious, for it provided that the Prince should be promoted to a higher rank once a fortnight and command a battalion by the end of the ten weeks!

Naturally he revolted against the iron discipline, and with the connivance of brother-officers found forbidden ways to pass his leisure time. Thus there began at the Curragh a liaison which was to have unfortunate repercussions when the Prince returned to Cambridge.

Meanwhile, after he had learned to manage a brigade, the Prince left Ireland on a secret visit to Germany. There he was to meet Princess Alexandra, the eldest daughter of Prince Christian (afterwards King Christian IX) of Denmark.

Although Queen Victoria was prejudiced against Denmark in favour of Germany, and especially against Prince Christian's family – whom she considered rather 'fast' and rather too boisterous for her – she recognized the need for an early and stable marriage for the Prince of Wales, who since his eighteenth birthday had, of course, been eligible to succeed to the throne as King (that is, without a Regency) should his mother die.

The Prince had known of Alexandra's existence since his days in Richmond Park when he used to visit relations – the old Duchess of Cambridge and her daughter Princess Mary Adelaide, who was to become the mother of Queen Mary – in their home at Kew not far away.

It was there that he first saw a miniature of Princess Alexandra. He was then sixteen and the Princess Alexandra was fourteen. Bertie was greatly impressed by her beauty and her sweetness of expression, but mistakenly assumed that she was betrothed to someone else.

Now, in the autumn of 1861, he was being quietly pushed towards the girl whom he would have chosen to marry, anyhow, given a free choice.

Six or eight suitable Protestant princesses had been considered. Most of them were Germans. Alexandra was number five on the list to start with, but one newspaper, alert to what was going on, considered her to be the most eligible.

Three women had a big hand in the final decision to marry Bertie to 'Alix', as she became known in the Royal Family.

One was his sister, the Princess Royal, who arranged the German meeting. The second was Countess von Hohenthal, who was married to Augustus Paget, the Queen's new Minister to Copenhagen. The third was the Duchess of Cambridge, who wrote: "It would be surprising if we women couldn't arrange this match."

An essential preliminary to marriage, of course, was the selection of a home for the Prince and his bride. And all this was happening at a time when the Prince Consort said that Bertie needed a proper home of his own in London.

Marlborough House was the right one, a *very* happy home, and handy for the Palace, but his father felt that, because his son was so fond of the country, he needed also a country home, further away than White Lodge at Richmond, where he could escape the constant strain of his position.

It was his father (a man of brilliant inspiration) who searched for a home for him and, by his careful management of the Duchy of Cornwall estates during the minority of his son (who was born Duke of Cornwall), provided the funds to buy it.

At this time the Prince Consort heard of a house in Norfolk, in a very sheltered district. It was screened by woodland surroundings, stood in a pretty park, and was known as Sandringham House.

This part of Norfolk is a warm corner in a cold county, but the house was small; it had only about ten bedrooms then, but there was plenty of room for additions. The parkland surrounding it, and leading to the little church, had several houses in it, and these could be used for ladies-in-waiting, equerries, visitors and such.

Sandringham House belonged to a man called Spencer Cowper. It was mentioned in Domesday Book, where it is referred to as Sand-Dersingham House. It had great charm.

Prince Albert felt that Sandringham could be highly suitable for his son because it was far from the crowds and was what he called a "homely" house.

Father and son went down to see it together. They fell in love with it.

At Sandringham the great joy was that there was no hallmark of the Crown, for whatever may be said of Buckingham Palace, Windsor Castle and Marlborough House, they do bear this mark!

The mansion was small at the moment, would need building on to, for staff quarters would be required. But as far as the young Prince was concerned it was Liberty Hall. It had

The Prince of Wales and
Princess Alice

The young Prince and his
tutors at Oxford

Prince Edward and Princess Alexandra with Queen Victoria
after their marriage in 1863

a lovely loneliness, away from the world, and some of the very best shooting in England, which was so desirable.

His father was enchanted with it too.

The Prince of Wales was one of the best shots in the land, and his father knew that he needed somewhere to enjoy this pastime. The Royal Family had always adored dear Balmoral, but it was too far away and there were times of year when it was not so good.

Bertie was not fond of Buckingham Palace, preferring Windsor Castle and the Great Park, and to him it seemed that Sandringham was a dream house.

The records of this fine house since it became a royal home have not been too kind, for much has gone wrong there.

The Prince of Wales's youngest son died there soon after he had been christened Alexander John Charles Albert – the first English prince to be named John since Henry IV's reign. The name and the tragedy were repeated in 1919 when King George V's youngest son John died on the estate at the age of thirteen.

Between these two deaths came the tragedy of King George V's elder brother, who was Heir to the Throne and known as 'Prince Collar and Cuffs' because of his very long wrists and neck. This young Prince, created Duke of Clarence, died at Sandringham from influenza in the New Year of 1892.

It was there that King George V died in the New Year of 1936 while the Royal Family were spending the Christmas holidays there. And it was there, when the New Year of 1952 was little more than a month old, that his son George VI died in his sleep after he had seen his daughter, the present Queen Elizabeth II, off on the first stages of her tour of the Southern Commonwealth, which had to be broken off in East Africa when her father, a king adored by all, passed peacefully away.

Yet the house is kindly and friendly; it has always been home to generations of the Royal Family, somewhere where they could do as they liked. Possibly some of the happiest holidays of their lives have been spent there.

Prince Albert picked on the place for this very lively young Prince of Wales. Queen Victoria was interested in it, and thought it would be a splendid quiet home for the Prince and his future bride when they wanted to get away from the stir of things.

It might be far away but it could be reached fairly quickly, for the marvel of the steam engine had changed life in the country for so many, and there were fast trains down there.

Sandringham enchanted the Prince of Wales.

"I think I am the luckiest fellow in all the world," he said.

In this life it is always the unexpected that happens. A lot was to happen before Bertie and Alix were married.

After meeting Alexandra and her mother, Queen Louise, in the cathedral at Speier – an 'accidental' encounter quietly arranged by the Duchess of Cambridge – the Prince of Wales returned to Cambridge.

Sandringham had been acquired. But, although nobody knew it at this time, the great tragedy of Queen Victoria's life lay just ahead of her.

Suddenly trouble caught up with the Prince of Wales.

The storm broke soon after he had celebrated his twentieth birthday on 9th November 1861. "May God bless and protect him and may he turn out well!" wrote the Queen.

Then a notorious gossip disclosed to the Prince Consort at Windsor that the Prince of Wales had formed a liaison with an actress!

He had been warned by his father to be careful, to avoid 'scrapes', which he could fall into very easily – "and those in authority," he added, "know everything there is to know about you."

This was only too true, but Bertie had arrived at a dangerous time in his career when he thought he knew best. He certainly intended to enjoy life at Cambridge, for it might be the last big chance that he got! But, of course, he did find it more difficult that he had expected. The masters knew everything.

"Just a bit fossilized," was the way that he put it, and, sooner rather than later, he realized, as he said to his friends – "a chap can't be the Prince of Wales *all* the time!"

General Bruce was a hard driver, and he laid down the law. It was a great contrast to life in the States, as the boy knew. "I've been king of the castle too long," he told himself ruefully – and he now had to obey the rules, and just do what he was told!

Perhaps this transition stage had come somewhat too soon for him. He had hardly recovered from his visit to Ireland and Germany before he found himself eating humble pie.

In pursuit of his illicit romance, on one occasion he did make a dash for London, because he very much wanted to see this girl. The family would never know that he had been, for he had arranged the whole thing remarkably well – so he thought! – and he got into the train with the gay optimism of youth in his heart, all out for a good time! He travelled as an ordinary young man, and thought he was conducting the affair with bright ability, until he got to the London terminus.

Unfortunately, somebody else knew.

He was met at Liverpool Street Station by a couple of Court officials (sent from the palace to do this) and there was no nonsense about it! They did not care what his excuse was! He was being put aboard the next train back to Cambridge, and he would be met at the other end. This was hardly encouraging!

It was an indignity which made him furiously angry, for it hardly fitted in with his triumphant arrivals in America, and there was nothing that he could do to change it! He had just to sit there for the return journey, seething with rage, and not even able to send a message to the girl who was concerned. But it *did* teach him how a future king was treated at Cambridge University and how he was guarded against himself.

He did not think it funny!

He had adapted himself to the life, and knew that he had to learn a lot. Ahead of him lay difficulties, and he would

probably have to marry to order, which was *not* his idea at all!
He found girls particularly appealing, and he was remarkably
clever at getting to know the better-looking ones! But, as his
tutor once explained to him: "This is one of the reasons for
good-looking girls coming to live in Cambridge."

He got what he called "a foot loose", and did rather well,
but although he had no idea of it, at this time all sorts of plans
were being made for his future.

At home it was the right moment to come to some
conclusion about his marriage. This thought had worried both
his parents for some while. He lived in the era of the 'arranged
wedding' – the wives of both George IV and William IV had
been chosen for them, and Victoria had been expected to
marry Prince Ernest, but had selected his brother. She had
been fortunate for she married the man she really loved.

Naturally she did not want an arranged marriage for her
son, but he was not in the position to choose for himself. She
knew that he was always having affairs, and now they sought
the most suitable princess to share his throne when the hour
came.

There were few suitable princesses available. The matter of
faith was the main worry. They felt it would be a good thing
when he left Cambridge (and she was most disturbed about
the reports that he was getting) and could settle down.

"I think that applies to every young man at the
universities," her husband said. "You must allow a little
sowing of wild oats."

"But it is entirely *wrong* for a Prince of Wales."

"It may be all *wrong*, but it is the natural thing for him to do
and there is no need to worry."

The Queen carefully pondered the list of eligible brides for
Bertie. She had to be *particularly* careful, for her eldest
daughter's marriage to the future Emperor of Germany had
not turned out well! Once they had been so much in love at
Balmoral, but now everything had gone wrong. His parents
were most demanding, they did not like the English princess,
and showed it, and it had worried the Queen very much
indeed.

The Prince Consort had gone over to Germany to "have it out with them", and it had not helped! Obviously Fritz was afraid of his parents, and then the trouble over the heir's crushed right arm had been blamed on the poor little Princess.

There were a great number of princesses in Europe at that time, but the majority of them were Catholics. The Queen was troubled about it. It was perhaps remarkable that her choice of Princess Alexandra of Denmark so completely reflected her son's attitude.

They got a picture of the young girl, and most certainly, she really was very beautiful, there could be no arguments about that, but there was one great disadvantage, her family were badly off, how would they ever afford the enormous expense of a wedding of the kind necessary for the Prince of Wales?

They understood that the young Princess was very slightly deaf, nothing to worry about, but occasionally she did not catch a remark and that was a drawback in society. They actually consulted with a famous aurist before they went further into the matter! He said that he thought the condition would not degenerate very much.

The name of Princess Alexandra of Denmark was promoted from number five to the top of the list, and his father thought that it was very urgent that Bertie should marry a really very pretty girl. Looks meant a lot to this young man! Perhaps her greatest advantage was that she was a Protestant, and so far religious complications had been very difficult to cope with.

The Queen was one of those women who went into every detail, leaving nothing to chance. The Prince Consort thought that she was the right girl, charming, so reports said, and really very very pretty. The Queen had thought of asking her over on a visit to Windsor Castle, but this, the Prince Consort thought, would be a mistake. To the girl it could only seem that she had come here on approval.

The Prince of Wales had several love affairs at Cambridge, yet the one which brought his career to a climacteric seems to have eluded the authorities – who probably thought it would peter out and therefore took no further action – until gossip in the London clubs brought matters to a head.

He was in love with an actress!

Victoria wanted a fine king to follow her, although in her heyday as Queen she considered Bertie more as an adjunct to the throne than as its eventual inheritor.

She idolized her country, and she was concerned because, as she thought, her heir was none too reliable. He had had the best education that the combined wit of her numerous counsellors – including her beloved Albert – had been able to devise, with the advantage of residence at the two ancient universities.

When she heard of some of his peccadillos his kind father said they only represented a stage through which most young men pass.

"All of us have the right to enjoy our springtime," he said, genially.

"But he is everlastingly doing something ridiculous!" the Queen protested.

Her fears seemed to be justified when, a week after his twentieth birthday, his love affair with the actress came to light and Prince Albert wrote to his son "with a heavy heart" on a subject which had caused him "the greatest pain I have yet felt in this life".

As we have seen, the affair began at the Curragh camp. Bruce – on the Prince Consort's orders – immediately challenged the Prince of Wales with the "deception" he had practised upon him as his "governor" by giving him no inkling of his passion for this woman!

The Prince was contrite. He explained that at first he had resisted the blandishments of fellow-officers and had tried not to get involved with the actress. But he had given in to temptation. Yes, alas, the story was true.

But, persisted the Prince, the affair was now all over for good. He refused, however, to name the officers who had got him into trouble.

The Prince Consort did not press the point.

"The past is past," he wrote to Bertie. "You have now to deal with the future."

He urged the Prince of Wales to concentrate his mind upon contracting an early marriage. He must "fight a valiant fight". He *must* not, he *dare* not, be lost: the consequences for his country and for the world would be too dreadful!

The Prince Consort's state of mind can be imagined from these rather extravagant phrases. He was nevertheless a loving and discerning parent, and he followed up his written advice by taking a special train to Cambridge and forgiving his son in person.

They had a down-to-earth interview at Madingley Hall – all repentance on the one side and all forgiveness on the other. But by this time, largely because of overwork in numerous causes and not merely because of his worry about his son, the Prince Consort was feeling thoroughly seedy.

According to Queen Victoria, his exhaustion was caused by Bertie – "who mistook the road during their walk" at Cambridge. In the light of after-events, this gave her an opportunity to blame her son endlessly for the tragedy which was now to overtake the royal House of Saxe-Coburg and Gotha.

In fact, the Prince Consort had developed a "shockingly bad cold" – the first diagnosis. There had been a spell of surprisingly hard weather for November, and soon a number of people went down under it.

Then political trouble – very menacing trouble – flared up and Britain came close to war with the United States. The Prince Consort was considerably worried, for he could not see a way out.

America was a mighty force, admirably armed.

For two whole nights the Prince Consort did not go to bed as he racked his brains to find some possible way out of the crisis.

In addition, Albert had to contend with two personal worries in addition to his concern about the Prince of Wales. His youngest son, the haemophiliac Prince Leopold, was ill, and the Prince Consort's cousin, King Pedro V of Portugal, whom the Prince of Wales had visited on at earlier overseas trip, had died at the age of twenty-five. The Prince Consort loved Pedro "like a son" and was grieved beyond measure by his untimely death.

Albert had also gone to a great deal of trouble, which involved some personal strain, to arrange details of another big overseas tour for Bertie, this time to the Holy Land, as soon as he left Cambridge.

Then, when he heard about the Prince of Wales's 'scrape' with the actress, the Prince Consort confessed in a letter to the Princess Royal:

"I am at a very low ebb. Much worry and great sorrow."

He did not go into details. But his "very heavy catarrh, headaches and pains in the limbs" portended, in fact, the onset of typhoid fever and not, what was originally thought, rheumatic fever.

Yet so virile was his spirit that when someone urged him to rest he stressed the danger of the looming war with the United States and replied sharply:

"This is not the time to rest. The lives of perhaps thousands depend on what I do *now*!"

It was in this state of near-exhaustion that he had travelled to Cambridge to see Bertie. It must have been one of the coldest days of the year, but against his doctors' wishes he went. His son's future was far more important, he said. He *must* go.

Then, perhaps for the first time, he wondered whether the Queen had been right when she had said that there *was* something of the old Georges in the boy! Bertie liked women, but he could not afford to behave as he was doing, for he was the future King. Undoubtedly this nonsense had got to stop!

It is quite possible that the Prince of Wales's extremely successful tour of North America had gone to his head a little. He was a very clever young man, he found it easy to do things that others found difficult, and overseas he had learned for the first time the sweet uses of power!

On his return from Cambridge the Prince Consort went straight to bed; he had developed a most hacking cough! He could not sleep through it. Very soon his anxiety for his son faded before his own anxiety for his own condition. The doctors who attended him had been in the Queen's service for years, and were all old men. She trusted them.

Her second daughter, the Princess Alice, was frantic with anxiety about her father. She was most interested in nursing, and saw through her mother's attachment to these old doctors, for she read a lot about the advance in medicine and the new discoveries. The Queen was happy that the Prince Consort was having the very best treatment, but his daughter felt that the old men tending him were out of date, and that he was in a far worse condition than they said. She wanted a second opinion. She said so.

The Queen had no idea that anything really serious was the matter, her doctors had no wish to alarm her, and it was far too late in the day when, at last, she listened to her daughter and a far more modern specialist was called in. By this time there was no hope for the Prince's life.

Albert was the power behind the throne, the man who had taught Victoria how to be the Queen, guiding her patiently through. When she was told that he could not live, she stared at the doctor in real agony! The thought of his death had never for a moment occurred to her, and she could not believe what he said!

The Prince of Wales returned hurriedly from Cambridge, for his sister had sent for him. He was bemused with horror when he heard that his father was dying! He was even more horror-stricken when he recognized that the man had been too ill to make that journey down to Cambridge, one of the coldest towns in England. In his agony he felt that he was at fault! It was a set of circumstances which had linked themselves together, one after the other, and brought them to this dreadful climax.

The hour came when the weeping family clustered around the dying Prince's bed, where he lay unconscious. When he ceased to breathe, poor Victoria could not believe that this was true! She had never for a single moment thought of life without him. She stared at him with the tears pouring down her face, and it was her eldest son who put an arm round her, and very gently led her away.

She collapsed in the next room, and ultimately they got her to her own suite, prostrate with grief. It was only her profound dedication to the Crown that brought her back to duty, for she must *not* forget that she was the Queen!

But in those few hours she was so appallingly stricken that she changed completely. The girl had died with her husband; she was now an *old* woman! For the first time for years she wept in her son's arms, he promising to help her in every way that he could, and well aware of her difficulties. He told her tomorrow it would be easier, she must not give way!

She turned to him, the tears pouring down her cheeks, and she said pathetically: "There is nobody left to call me Victoria."

That was true!

She recovered, of course, because this is something that people have to do, even if they feel terrible. But her son could hardly believe that this was the woman he had known last week, for she had changed so much. He promised to do everything that he could (and he meant this); for a passing moment, apparently, she had faith in him, and she did let him write some of the letters for her. But that did not last! She seems never to have trusted him entirely, and for no reason.

To Uncle Leopold in Belgium she wrote and told him how truly dreadful she felt about this loss.

But [she wrote] I am only outwardly separated, and this can only be for a time.

Little did she know that it would be *forty years*, during which she would quite deliberately waste her eldest son's genius for kingship, and would stay a background Queen, never doing very much, but never taking his advice in any possible way.

"I would help you," he told her.

She looked at him coldly, "If you had behaved yourself as a Prince should do, your poor father would never have gone down to Cambridge and would still be here with us," was what she told him.

There was no answer to that.

7

Marriage to Alexandra

The Prince, by breeding, background and education, was well qualified to help Queen Victoria in every possible way, but at no time did she avail herself of his assistance in any significant way.

She did, of course, let him carry out a large number of engagements which she had no heart to discharge herself, but she kept him severely at arm's length when it came to sharing any of her State duties.

Of course, the Prince of Wales realized that sooner or later he would have to marry, and it was quite likely that the girl would be chosen for him and would not be his choice. That is what he thought. There had been so much of it in the Royal Family before his time.

He also had an idea that Uncle Leopold, the great brain on whom the Queen and Prince Albert had always relied, would help finalize the choice of a bride for him.

Uncle Leopold, who had been King of the Belgians since 1831, was an extremely kind and wise old man, and he it was who privately reduced the list of possible princesses eligible to wear the Consort's crown of England down to a short list of three.

Like the three matchmaking ladies already mentioned, Leopold thought that the daughter of the Royal House of Denmark – Princess Alexandra – was the most likely candidate.

She was quite the prettiest princess in Europe at the time, brought up very quietly, for her family were not rich, so much so that up to the time of her marriage she shared a bleak little bedroom with her favourite sister Dagmar (afterwards Empress of Russia).

Alexandra and her brothers and sisters were born at the Yellow Palace on the Amaliegade. The owner of this rather dilapidated mansion was their father, then Prince Christian of Schleswig-Holstein-Sonderburg-Glucksburg, a captain of the King's Guard.

This Christian was the fourth of the six sons of Duke Frederick of Schleswig-Holstein, but the family fortunes had declined during the Napoleonic wars.

The lives of Princess Alexandra and her future husband were to be darkened by a political wrangle and war over Schleswig-Holstein. These two duchies had for centuries been ruled by the parent family of the Danish kings, the Oldenburgs.

The Schleswigers considered themselves to be Danes, but the Holsteiners wanted independence and looked to the neighbouring German states for support in their claim.

This feud was to be a thorn in European relations for the best part of the lives of the future King Edward and Queen Alexandra.

Actually the Danish Crown eventually passed to Prince Christian through his wife Princess Louise of Hesse-Cassel. They were married in 1842, and by the time Alexandra became engaged to Albert Edward they had six children, all born before their parents ascended the Danish throne.

As these children played a large part in the lives of the future King and Queen of England it is worth looking to see what they became.

The eldest, Frederick, was to succeed his father as King of Denmark in 1906. Alexandra was the second child, born on 1 December 1844. Between 1845 and 1859 were born William, who became King George I of Greece; Dagmar ('Minnie'), who became Russia's Empress Marie Fedorovna; another sister, Thyra; and finally a brother, Valdemar.

Because of their large families and the royal alliances which sprang from them King Christian IX and Queen Victoria were known as "the grandparents of Europe".

Of course, Queen Victoria already knew a good deal – some of it false – about the Christians and the 'fast' life which she thought they led, long before she cast an approving eye upon Princess Alexandra as a potential daughter-in-law. There had even been *divorces* in that Danish family!

Christian had attended Queen Victoria's coronation as envoy of the Danish King. At that time he could well have been a rival to Prince Albert of Coburg for Victoria's hand, but the Duchess of Kent – the young Queen's domineering mother – stepped in and snubbed Christian without mercy. She much preferred Albert (she, too, was a Coburg). Besides, this Christian was so poor that he scarcely had a decent suit of clothes to his back!

The Christian family, contrary to many of the reports which had reached Windsor, nevertheless had a rather Spartan upbringing in their decayed little palace. Their household was certainly run on frugal lines. There were few luxuries. On his pay as an army captain Prince Christian could hardly afford them.

But he was a great man for 'physical jerks' and the cult of health. He used to drill Alexandra and her brothers and sisters in all kinds of muscle-building exercises. He even taught them to cartwheel.

In the most natural way possible Alexandra, when she was Princess of Wales, used to entertain trusted friends at Marlborough House by somersaulting and turning cartwheels on the drawing-room floor, remarking merely that it was "only a matter of speed".

No doubt it was this boisterous kind of education, more Scandinavian than Victorian, that so upset the august Queen when her emissaries reported these strange goings-on at Amaliegade and the summer palace at Bernstorff, at Rumpenheim – where the Danish royals and their German and Russian relations used to forgather for regular 'reunions' – and later at Fredensborg, the Danish royal palace.

In their youth the members of the Danish Royal Family were allowed to jump up and down on Queen Louise's sofas until they smashed the springs. The Danish Queen could not hear the clatter because she was deaf (Alexandra inherited this deafness), but she liked young people to enjoy life.

This could never have happened at Windsor!

However, Queen Victoria was prepared to set aside her doubts and scruples if Uncle Leopold recommended Alexandra as a suitable wife for Bertie and a suitable daughter-in-law for herself.

But there was probably one thing that made up her mind more than anything else in Alexandra's favour.

The Prince Consort – "the Beloved One", as he would be known throughout Victoria's long widowhood – had approved of Alexandra before he died. He had, in fact, been warmed by the Countess Walburga's description of the Danish princess as "a half-open rosebud, so simple and childlike in everything".

Victoria was therefore in a mood to receive everything that Leopold and her other advisers and informants told her about the Danish princess with an open heart, especially as The Beloved One would have agreed with his uncle.

The girl spoke some English already, but not very well as yet, though this was not important, for she had a breath-taking beauty which would catch any man's eye.

Meanwhile the Prince of Wales was carrying out all those engagements which the Queen, in her grief over Albert, was refusing. To friends the Prince said, and with truth, "Here I am, doing Mama's job for her, being worked to death, and not paid a bob for it!"

Although he was not aware of all the intricate little moves being made to bring him and Alexandra together, he certainly was aware of his mother's growing dislike – almost hatred – for him since the Prince Consort's death.

She repeatedly referred to his affair with the actress at Cambridge as 'Bertie's fall' – she would not let the subject drop – and she told the Princess Royal that she could not bear the sight of him. She felt a shudder every time she looked at him.

There is no doubt that for various reasons the Queen was not herself. Apart from the anguish over her husband's death, she had reached what the biographer of King Edward called "the most trying period in a woman's life", which later historians have interpreted as the menopause. This undoubtedly increased her feelings of unreasoning hostility, almost loathing, towards her bewildered son, who would have done almost anything to please her.

The situation was temporarily saved by a decision to carry out the Prince Consort's plans to send his son and heir on a long tour of the Holy Land. It was accepted that he should marry Princess Alexandra, should his mother approve, after his return several months later.

General Bruce and Canon Arthur Stanley, an Oxford professor and an expert on Palestine, accompanied the Prince of Wales, who travelled first to Vienna to see the Emperor Franz Josef. By the time he reached Egypt the Prince was in cheerful spirits and wanted to shoot crocodiles in the Nile rather than inspect "tumbledown temples".

The Prince rode horseback to Jerusalem, and during this interval grew a wonderful beard, the foundation of the beard which is an essential feature of his image both as Prince of Wales and as King.

After a thorough exploration of Palestine, the Prince – who had covered the sea part of the journey in the royal yacht *Osborne* – went to Turkey, where to his delighted surprise he found a most warm letter from the Queen awaiting him.

Presumably she had thought a good deal about her son after he had left and wondered whether she had not been too hard on him, though she took a long time to push into the background the "painful subject" of his affair with that actress.

Bruce recorded when the Prince read the Queen's letter: "I wish you could have seen the face of the Prince of Wales when he read the Queen's letter to him. It was actually beaming

The Prince of Wales and his family

Lady Brooke, afterwards Frances, Countess of Warwick, in 1889

with pleasure ... It is a hopeful feature in his character that he has a strong love of approbation.''

It was during this tour that his advisers noticed that the Prince displayed those gifts of diplomacy which were to stand him, and his country, in such good stead in after-years.

The royal party travelled via Greece and up through France to Paris, where the Prince bought gifts for Princess Alexandra.

On his return he was greeted with demonstrations of great affection by his mother. "I was much upset on seeing him and feeling his beloved father was not there to welcome him back,'' she wrote ...

"He is very improved in every respect, so kind and nice to the younger children, more serious in his ways and views, and most anxious for his marriage.''

The only black spot was the death of General Bruce, who contracted fever in Palestine and collapsed in Paris. He was fifty-nine. His successor, General Sir William Knollys, was to form a lifelong friendship with the Prince.

"Most anxious for his marriage ...'' Those were the Queen's words. And so Bertie was.

But while the preparations were still going forward he still had to work hard at the royal 'trade', as his mother secluded herself at Windsor and for months after the Prince Consort's death would not even go out.

Whereas she would not give Bertie a 'bob' (shilling, now five pence) for the job, his father had always been extremely generous with cheques, always ready to help his son if he was in a muddle. But Victoria on such occasions protested that she herself was hard up (which was quite untrue and he knew it): she could at times be extremely mean.

"It isn't all beer and skittles being a Queen's son, and worse if you are her heir,'' Bertie told his friends. He longed for someone to share his burden.

The Queen was now intensely interested in the subject of Bertie's marriage. She had heard a great deal about Alexandra – how she made her own dresses and how her mother, Queen Louise, had vowed: "I shall bring my children up in sackcloth that they may later wear the purple more gracefully!"

The Princess Royal had assured her mother that Alexandra seemed to be "highly suitable for Bertie".

But his second sister – after an appeal from her brother – told her mother that the Prince was working too hard and needed a respite.

The Queen listened to all this, then swept it all aside, saying, as she always did:

"Oh, he is so young! It doesn't fatigue him at all, and he needs something to do. I am shattered by my great grief," and she took refuge in tears.

"But he *is* worked too hard, Mama," persisted Princess Alice.

"A son *has* to serve. It is high time that he learnt his role as Prince of Wales and does it properly," – and the Queen's voice was cold.

Uncle Leopold's advice about Princess Alexandra helped to counterbalance all this. He was a most loyal, kind man and she could trust him implicitly.

When he wrote of Alexandra's beauty he added: "This ought to help you, for you know that Bertie admires good looks."

At this time the Queen was greatly troubled by the condition of the other Leopold, her youngest son. She had always hoped that he would recover from the malady with which he had been born, and although she kept telling herself that so far, so good, she was terrified lest he would have some awful accident and bleed to death.

[Leopold grew up and married Princess Helen of Waldeck, but in 1884 what the Queen had always feared for him happened! He went on a visit to France, where he slipped on some marble stairs, falling and cutting himself badly. He literally bled to death. It was the one thing his distracted mother had always felt *must* come, something she dared not speak about, but which, in 1861-62, must have added considerably to her anxiety at this time of mourning for her Albert].

Naturally the Queen was extremely anxious to meet the bride-to-be. She had the idea, like a lot of mothers, that honest marriage would put an end to her eldest son's flirtatiousness, which had caused her some considerable distress at times. She had always thought it to be quite wrong.

By this time her grief and suffering had prematurely aged her. In those days women quite willingly became old, and Victoria made no attempt to evade time. She prayed now earnestly for a happy marriage for her son and, when the time came, for sons to follow him to the throne of England.

But there were certain formalities first. It was believed that the Prince Consort's brother Ernest, Duke of Coburg, who had been a rival for Victoria's hand, had written to Alexandra's mother about the actress affair. The Queen suggested to the Princess Royal that the British ambassador in Copenhagen should let Louise know the truth.

No doubt the Christians took it all with great good humour as a youthful escapade, but the Queen wanted it known that the Prince of Wales "*would* make a steady husband" and that she looked to his future wife "as being his Salvation, for that he was very domestic and longed to be at home". In any case, the Queen thought that since he had returned from his overseas tour he was "immensely improved".

Then the Queen set out to visit King Leopold at his palace at Laeken, outside Brussels. She travelled incognito as the Countess of Balmoral.

She had two purposes. One was to visit those places where the beloved Albert had spent his childhood and, by recalling those happy memories, in some way to assuage her sorrow and to ease the burden of that "dreadful, dreadful cross" which she said was killing her.

The other was happier. It was to meet Princess Alexandra. Up to then the Queen had been able to judge of her future daughter-in-law only through photographs and reports. She wanted to see her in the flesh.

Alexandra and her sister Dagmar travelled with their parents from Ostend, where they had been staying, and Alexandra made an instant and unforgettable impression on the sad little Queen, who praised her loveliness – "such a beautiful refined profile, and quiet ladylike manner".

By this time the Queen was using the royal 'we', for she wished everybody to know that when she spoke she was speaking both for herself *and* for her dead Albert.

Should Alexandra accept "our son", she told the Christians, she hoped she would do so with all her heart. What could the Christians reply except that they hoped the Prince of Wales would feel the same about their daughter?

"Alexandra will be *the* Queen for England," Victoria kept telling herself after Bertie had proposed to the Danish princess at Laeken – "I still feel as if I was in a dream," he told his mother. "I fell in increasing love towards her every moment."

He particularly touched his mother by his references to his dead father. "I told her how *very* sorry I was that she could never know dear Papa. She said she regretted it deeply and hoped he would have approved of my choice. I told her that it had always been his greatest wish ..."

The Prince of Wales "frankly avowed" to his august parent that he "did not think it possible to love a person" as he loved Alexandra. She was so kind and good and, he felt sure, would make his life a happy one. "I only trust that God will give me strength to do the same for her."

Their engagement was announced on 16th September 1862. It had some political undertones and did not go down at all well in Germany, then still in the throes of her dispute with Denmark over Schleswig-Holstein. In Denmark, of course, it was regarded as a slap in the eye for the Germans.

In fact, the British Government and people had no feelings one way or the other. Queen Victoria was pro-German because of her own family associations and, of course, her beloved daughter Vicky was married to the future German Emperor. And although she was cool towards the Danes she did not allow her feelings, or any political considerations, to take precedence over the real pleasure she felt in the betrothal of the Prince of Wales and Princess Alexandra. After all, she herself had married for love and could obviously tell that Bertie's feelings for his fiancée were genuine.

When the engagement was made public the Prince besought his mother to abandon the heaviest mourning.

The next step in the courtship had been for the Queen to invite Alexandra to visit Osborne and Windsor for a few weeks towards the end of the year. She wanted to have Alexandra to herself.

But she was still wearing black – indeed, she was to wear black to the end of her reign. It would give his future bride a happier picture of the country, said Bertie, if his mother were to wear something less depressing.

Victoria resolutely refused!

To his horror he then found that she was still insisting that every night her dead husband's evening clothes should be laid out for him in his dressing-room, and in the morning the suit that he would have worn that day!

The King of the Belgians tried to help the Prince in this matter, but nothing in the world could move the Queen. She would wear her mourning until the day that she died, and said, even at her son's wedding. Nothing would dissuade her!

The Queen wanted her future daughter-in-law to see her at home as she was. And she equally wanted to see Alexandra apart from her relations. She disliked the Christian family and their connections very much, and did not want Bertie to get caught up in their quarrel with Germany over the two duchies.

Alexandra did not like the idea of going to England 'on approval', so to speak, but the future throne of Great Britain was a rich prize and she had to do as she was told.

Meanwhile the Prince of Wales was sent away. His mother wished to see Alexandra *alone*. So from Coburg he travelled to Switzerland and then on to Marseilles for a Mediterranean cruise on the royal yacht *Osborne*.

His mother had asked the Princess Royal and her husband to go with him, especially as Vicky was being criticized by her enemies at the Prussian Court for helping to get her brother married to a Dane. It happened, too, that Germany was in ferment over Bismarck's policy of Prussian expansionism.

After visiting Tunis and Carthage, Sicily, Malta and Naples – where the Prince celebrated his twenty-first birthday – and a stay in Rome with his sister and her husband, Bertie managed to get a sight of Alexandra at Calais on her way home to Copenhagen.

He wanted to travel with her to Denmark, but the Queen was absolutely firm that in the present situation England must not be seen to be siding with Denmark – and she certainly did not want her son getting himself "entangled with *that* family", meaning the Christians.

But Alexandra during her visit to the Queen had made a great impression. The Queen was much taken by her simple, unaffected, frank, bright and cheerful manner – those were the adjectives she used to describe the girl – and she even went so far as to call her a "jewel" – one of those sweet creatures who seemed to "come from the skies to help and bless poor mortals and lighten for a time their path!"

The Princess also satisfied Parliament. She fulfilled all those conditions which, so Lord Palmerston told the Commons, the Government regarded as indispensable: she was young, handsome, well brought up – and a Protestant.

At this time Czar Alexander II of Russia was seeking Alexandra's hand for his heir. This may have played some part in making up everybody's mind! In the event the choice fell upon Alexandra's sister Dagmar.

There is, of course, far more work behind a royal marriage than a member of the public ever knows. Parliament raised the Prince of Wales's income from £60,000 to £100,000, while Alexandra was granted £10,000 a year with the guarantee of a further £20,000 if she were widowed while Victoria still lived.

Among his numerous activities the Prince Consort had found time to design an ambitious plan of renovations for

Marlborough House. These were now carried out, down to the very last detail.

The Prince of Wales – who had gone as far as Hanover, his German ancestors' kingdom, with Alexandra – now returned home. He was in time to join the Royal Family on what became an annual pilgrimage to the mausoleum at Frogmore on the anniversary of the Prince Consort's death, 14th December.

Once again the Queen found Bertie looking "much improved", although she wondered whether he had been properly "germanized".

She hoped, too, that Alexandra would rid her son of the cigar-smoking habit, as "beloved Albert so *highly* disapproved of it, which ought to be enough to deter Bertie from it". But she never did.

The wedding was arranged for 10th March 1863. Meanwhile gifts poured in from the European royalties. The Danes – with the sulky exception of the pro-German Holsteiners – raised a handsome dowry. And Alexandra was baptized with the rites of the Episcopal Church.

Three days before the wedding she set sail, the first time for a century that a princess of Denmark was to marry abroad. With her went her brother William and her sisters Dagmar and Thyra.

As they were about to leave the boiler of the steamship blew up with a loud bang, so the royal party had to transfer to another vessel which took them, via the Kiel Canal, to Antwerp.

There the new royal yacht *Victoria and Albert* took the royal party aboard for the voyage to England. But when she sailed into Gravesend (to be met, though rather late, by the Prince of Wales) the warships on escort duty were silent.

Not a gun was allowed to be fired in salute. Nor were the sailors permitted to shout loyal greetings. By the Queen's command the royal bride was to be received without any kind of official welcome because of the Court mourning for the Prince Consort!

This did not stop the townspeople of Gravesend and bystanders along the route to London roaring with delight and pleasure at their first glimpse of the incredibly beautiful Princess, in her mauve Irish poplin, with a cloak of sable-trimmed purple velvet and a white poked bonnet edged with rosebuds.

In the City of London the crowds, who had waited for a long time in snow and bitter winds, got out of hand. There were some ugly scenes.

One boy caught his head in the wheelspokes of the Princess's carriage, but Alexandra, with a dexterity which amazed the Prince of Wales, leaned over and extricated him – without injury to the boy, though she badly wrenched her shoulder in the process. Despite this she smiled bravely and carried on bowing and waving to the populace.

At last the royal party arrived at Windsor several hours late.

The exhausted and half-frozen Alexandra drooped into the Queen's arms like a "crumpled rose", and the Queen kissed her again and again. Then, feeling thoroughly desolate and sad, the Queen excused herself from family dinner.

Victoria did not really recover until the next day – the wedding eve – when she showed Alexandra over the Frogmore mausoleum and talked tearfully of the Prince Consort. "*He* gives you his blessing," said the Queen.

The Prince of Wales would have liked to have been married in Westminster Abbey, where many people could have feasted their eyes on his lovely bride, or in the Chapel Royal at St James's Palace, where his mother and his eldest sister, the Princess Royal, had been wed.

But the Queen was adamant and would not leave Windsor. For her the Chapel Royal was sacred to the memory of Albert. [This rule was not relaxed until the future King George V was married to Princess Mary of Teck in the Chapel Royal in 1893].

The marriage accordingly took place on 10th March 1863 in St George's Chapel. The Queen refused to appear herself.

This was most irritating of her. She was a widow, in deep mourning and frivolities of this sort did not fit in with that, she said. She could watch from a gallery, seeing, but unseen!

Her son said that she had a duty to her country, *and* to him. Vehemently she denied it. None could talk Victoria round when she had made up her mind. She was possibly one of the most determined women of her time, and her son knew this.

He had come to the conclusion that nobody could ever persuade Mama, and since his father's death he himself seemed to have lost any power that he might ever have had over her. Perhaps he had not had as much as he had supposed. Perhaps he had, in some ways, been indirectly responsible for his father's death. He tried to sum things up! He was now becoming far more popular than his mother was in the country – and she would not like *that*, as he knew. What does one do with Mama? he asked himself.

And when Mama is the Queen of England there is nothing that one *can* do, save grin and bear it, and this was what he *did* do.

The marriage had really been love at first sight. It had been the marvellous arrangement of King Leopold, and it had been beautifully done. I am sure the Prince of Wales never thought of it as a marriage of convenience at all.

The 10th March was a fine bright day! Only half the number of people who should have been asked to the ceremony could be got inside St George's Chapel, but apparently that was what the old Queen wanted. I think privately she hated any festivity when she was, as she once put it, so bitterly in mourning, and I think also that, with the shock of her husband's death, there had come to her a sort of shyness, and reluctance to meet the crowd! She had never had this as a girl, but, judging by her behaviour after this tremendous shock, I am sure she felt that she could not face them.

She had refused to take any part in the ceremony, though her son had implored her to do so. Once she made up her mind, she had always been the woman whom nobody and nothing would change. She might be the mother of the bridegroom, but she was not presenting herself in the chapel. She explained that she had made up her mind to slip quietly into a gallery in St George's Chapel, from which she could see, but not be seen herself!

She sat in Catherine of Aragon's box, which was draped in purple velvet and gold. Except for the Garter ribbon she was all in black.

The Prince argued with her. The marriage of the Heir to the Throne was an occasion which the Queen should attend, and in state. Nothing would change her! She would, she said, mourn Albert to the end, and this was what she intended to do.

She would *be* there, she promised, but no one would be able to stare at her, and that was what she wished.

The bride had been enchanted by the surprisingly big welcome that she had received in her new country; she had never seen such crowds before and she was now in a land that was highly confident, a country at peace with the world, and growing every day more powerful! After little Denmark, it *must* have been surprising the crowds that turned out, and the tremendously boisterous welcome that she received.

From her box above, the Queen saw her eldest daughter, come over from Germany and with her, her eldest son, whom the old Queen always said was "such a dear little boy". She was never to know how Kaiser Wilhelm II (as he became) turned on her country and launched into that ghastly war of 1914! Had she ever done, I think she would have killed him herself, for Victoria was nothing less than most violently patriotic.

The wedding was a magnificent ceremony, and Jenny Lind, the 'Swedish Nightingale', sang the Prince Consort's Chorale at which Victoria (mercifully hidden from the world), burst into tears! She did not even try to hide her grief from the ladies who were with her.

Suddenly, where the bridegroom stood, she thought she saw a coffin. She left the box abruptly but later returned.

None of this was the ceremony that the Prince of Wales had wanted, and, of course, without a doubt it *should* have been in London, and the Queen *should* have appeared properly at it. The Prince Consort would have been the first man to urge this. But she was so grief-stricken that many of her subjects thought she had gone mad.

The Prince of Wales came into the Chapel wearing the Garter ribbon, and conducted by the heralds, and with the usual three best men. He walked up the nave to the chancel steps and then turned and bowed low to the high up window, where he knew that his mother would be sitting, though he knew perfectly well that nobody could actually see her.

When it was over the royal couple came down the aisle hand-in-hand, pausing for a moment before the high niche where they knew the Queen herself was sitting, and she actually thrust out a hand to wave to them! But her son had been most bitterly grieved for her, for not making a proper appearance for his sake. It seemed that she could not forget her sorrow for one half day.

There was, of course, a glorious reception, and the Queen supplied the best food and everything that she could do. The Eton boys had been given a special holiday for this great occasion (incidentally this is always the beginning of trouble) and they were determined to make the most of it, and do something thrilling to show how they felt about it.

The newly-married pair left Windsor Castle to drive to the Great Western station, to start their honeymoon at Osborne when the Etonians rushed out beside the carriage. Lord Randolph Churchill (Winston Churchill's father, and with much the same spirit) led the party, and the boys managed to unharness the horses, then got in between the shafts, and dragged the happy couple to the station.

Unfortunately, when they got there, in the thrill of the moment (for it was going even better than they had ever expected) they broke down the palisades, and had to pay for this later, much to their parents' fury, when the bills were sent in to them.

Nobody would ever know how the old Queen really felt about this marriage, though apparently she did like her very beautiful young daughter-in-law and admired her looks. But of course, she had never given the Prince of Wales his due, and now it was fairly certain that she never would. He tried to get her up to London, and out and about again, as she should have been, but no! She sought her eternal mourning for her dead Prince. Buckingham Palace was practically shut down, and although she liked the young Princess of Wales, she never really warmed to her son. The country was getting more than a little sick of this eternal mourning, and began to say so, but she plodded on in semi-retirement, and obviously she intended doing this until she died!

"What is she being paid for?" some asked. "After all, it is *our* money. Why should we pay her for doing nothing?"

Her eldest son was of quite another type. He would go anywhere, and do anything, also he would talk to anybody and was most friendly. Victoria was always on her dignity.

The time had now come when the disapproval of the country must have reached even Victoria herself, for the newspapers were not too polite to her, "Why doesn't she earn her money?" they asked! There had been a time in her life when she would have blazed back in a fury, but now she just sat down and cried, which was no help!

"Nobody can do anything with Mama," was the despairing way that the Prince of Wales summed it all up, and maybe he had got something there.

8

"I am the Queen!"

As the story of Edward unfolds Queen Victoria seems to lose a little in stature – and this may yet be the verdict of history, that she was not as great as some earlier historians made her out to be. Great people have their petty side, and the great Queen was no exception. Of course, her inconsolable grief for Albert – the feeling that she might not have done as much for him as she might when she had the opportunity – distorted her outlook, and Edward was a convenient target for her lacerated emotions. She resented his popularity while she did nothing at that time to improve her own standing with the public.

For instance, this habit of hers, of having Albert's clothes laid out by his valet every night, and having The Beloved One's room maintained as though he were still alive, preyed on Edward. When he protested against these macabre practices she retorted coldly: "I *am* the Queen!" She would brook no argument from anyone, least of all from her son. No one knew better than Edward that the Queen *is* the Queen. "It would be terribly sad if it were not so utterly wrong," he told Alexandra, who sympathized with him and to whom he turned in his darker hours for the consolation which, despite his waywardness, she never withheld.

The new Princess of Wales, even the Queen had to admit, was unique: she had never known anyone so beautiful in the family before. Alexandra had masses of glorious hair and very beautiful eyes that twinkled like stars when she was happy.

The Prince of Wales prayed that he would never bring tears to them.

The Queen hoped that, now that he had married quite the prettiest princess in Europe, he would give up having those promiscuous sex affairs which had been such a constant worry to her. He should settle down for good.

But the Prince of Wales was no settler-down!

He had a fascination for, and was fascinated by beautiful women all his life. Somehow Princess Alexandra understood him completely – after all, she had come from a very broad-minded family – and she was never really jealous.

In fact, she accepted his loves and, up to a point, was as friendly with them as convention permitted. She never tried to tie him to her apron-strings, as his mother would have done, and there were even times when she laughed about his affairs.

"You will always come back to me," she told him.

That was true. He always did. He kissed her and said: "That is a promise!" They were always in love throughout the whole forty-seven years of their married life together.

Marlborough House was, of course, the first house of which she had been mistress, and for that reason it seemed larger to her than any of the palaces back home in Denmark.

For the first time in her young life – she was eighteen – she did not have to make her own dresses or share a bedroom with a sister. It took her some time to get accustomed to having money and, of course, to take in her stride the love affairs of her romantically inclined husband. But she enjoyed entertaining, she loved dancing, and she found inexhaustible pleasure in giving and attending dinner parties.

One can understand how the old Queen at Windsor felt about all this, in her self-inflicted retirement; but, if she would not entertain, as the Prince said, somebody else had to do it for her.

When the news (for which the country had been waiting) came, and they were told that in March the next year they would have a child all the world hoped that it would be a prince.

Everybody prayed for a son to follow in his father's footsteps. The baby was to be born at Marlborough House, so it was arranged, but the best-laid schemes *can* go astray, even in royal circles. Two trained nurses were engaged for the month of February to be in good time, for the old days of Mrs Lily had gone for ever.

Alexandra had kept remarkably well and was going about quite a lot, not wilting on a sofa as was the custom of the day for expectant mothers or, as they were called, "ladies in a delicate state of health". In Denmark the birth of a baby was accepted as the most natural thing in the world.

Very early in January she went down to Windsor to pay a duty visit to the Queen, who accepted such calls as her right, and, indeed, insisted on them. It would be what the Prince of Wales called "one of Mama's talkings-to". The Princess of Wales did not seem to mind: she understood her mother-in-law.

The weather was bitterly cold. In the afternoon of 8th January the Princess was driven to Frogmore to watch the Prince of Wales and his friends play ice hockey on the frozen lake. She was all muffled up in a sleigh at the lakeside when suddenly her labour pains began without warning. She had complained previously of feeling "a little odd", but as the child was not expected for another two months she certainly did not recognize the symptoms.

The Queen's Windsor physician, Dr Brown, was the only medical man available in this crisis. He was rushed to the castle and, with the help of Lady Macclesfield – a royal confidante and herself the mother of a dozen children – he safely delivered Alexandra of a son, just three hours after she had been watching her husband cavorting on the ice.

Meanwhile a messenger sped to London to fetch down some of the clothes that had been prepared for the baby: he was wrapped in cotton wool until the messenger, accompanied by the doctors and nurses, returned with the layette.

The Prince was named Albert – the first of Victoria's descendants to be called after his revered grandfather – and Victor after the Queen, who elected to be his godmother. He was also named Christian after his maternal grandfather and Edward after his father, and in due course the Queen created him Duke of Clarence.

Queen Victoria took it all remarkably well, and for the moment seemed to put behind her the eternal mourning and sadness, for she occupied herself giving orders and doing what she could.

She herself had never rushed matters with her own children, for she had never delivered a baby in less than twelve hours, and was rather proud of her record.

In Germany at this time Bismarck, the new Chancellor – Prime Minister – had embarked on his policy of 'iron and blood'. Its ultimate aim was to unite the various German states under the leadership of Prussia. This process was to lead to the creation of the German Empire under Wilhelm I, a cousin of Prince Albert and the father of Bertie's brother-in-law Fritz.

One of the early steps in this campaign had the goal of depriving Denmark of at least one of the two duchies of Schleswig and Holstein which had been connected with Denmark for four centuries: King Christian was also duke of the two duchies, which formed Denmark's southern border with Germany. The dispute led to war.

It is important to recognize the significance this apparently trivial but complex dispute had on the future of Europe. The Prince of Wales took the view that a powerful state like Prussia should not oppress and threaten a small country like Denmark. In this he was as much influenced by his innate sense of 'fair play' as by the fact of his marriage to King Christian's lovely daughter. His opinion was shared by Lord Palmerston, the flamboyant Whig statesman. However, Palmerston had not been trusted by Prince Albert, and he had

Lillie Langtry

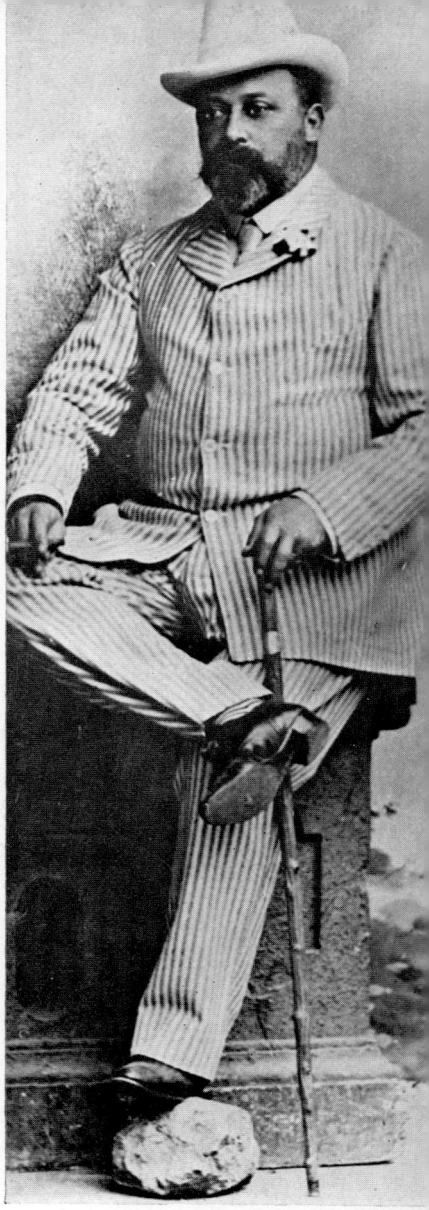

The King as sportsman and man about town. He set a new fashion
in hats by wearing what is now known as the homburg

upset Queen Victoria, not least in the way he acted after the Prince Consort's death. (He arrived at Court, where everything was draped in deadly black, wearing a brown overcoat, light grey trousers, green gloves and blue studs. Worse still, his whiskers were freshly dyed!). Palmerston's harsh and abrasive manner had already earned him the nickname of 'Lord Pumicestone'.

But it was not so much Lord Palmerston's and the Prince of Wales's sympathetic attitude towards the Danes that pained the Queen, and it was not only Victoria's pro-German outlook, springing from her family connections and the fact that her eldest daughter was married to the Prussian heir. It was that after the emotional stress to which she had been prey after Albert's death she devoutly wished for peace. Therefore she took no sides in the matter of Schleswig-Holstein.

Palmerston – who had, of course, been entranced by Princess Alexandra, as had so many of his fellow-countrymen – came down heavily on the side of the Danes and led them to think that Britain would help them, if necessary with arms. He did not like to see little countries being browbeaten by big ones.

But the Queen had no wish to become involved in war, especially after the unfortunate Crimean War just nine years earlier. Consequently Palmerston found that, with the exception of the Prince and Princess of Wales and their friends, he was speaking largely for himself and not for the Government or the general body of his compatriots, and certainly not for the Court or for Parliament.

When Prussia and Austria – who also claimed a certain sovereignty over the duchies – declared war on little Denmark it became obvious that Britain would not fight. In the subsequent fighting the two big allies naturally won an easy victory over Denmark, and Alexandra's country not only had to surrender her claims to the two duchies, but also had to pay a heavy war debt.

Victory gave Bismarck one of his principal objectives – the Kiel Canal, which was to be constructed as a further stage in the union of greater Germany, and it was to prove a great menace to Britain in the world war which the Prince of Wales's charming but unscrupulous and warlike nephew, Wilhelm II, was to be given the lion's share for starting in 1914.

At this time, too, certain domestic happenings were of great interest to the royal families of Britain and Denmark.

Alexandra's brother William had become King George I of the Hellenes and Dagmar had become betrothed to the Czarevitch Nicholas of Russia (on whose death before they were married she was to become the fiancée of his younger brother, the future Czar Alexander III). But Frederick, King Christian's heir and an Oxford graduate, had wanted to marry one of the Prince of Wales's young sisters, Helena. Victoria wished Helena to marry a German. In his rage King Christian complained: "They wound our most sacred feelings! That is typically English. They think of nothing but their own advantage, and never consult the heart." In fact, Helena married the ruler of Schleswig-Holstein – a bitter blow for the Danish Royal Family.

All this bitterness had filled Alexandra's cup to overflowing when, after the birth of the Duke of Clarence, she and her husband with the infant Prince visited Copenhagen. It was to be the first of forty visits which Alexandra was to pay to her homeland between her marriage and her accession to the throne in 1901, an average of one visit a year.

The Prince of Wales's mood can be summed up in a remark he made just before they left.

"This horrible war," he said of the attack on Denmark, "will be a stain for ever on Prussian history."

During the voyage the royal yacht had to enter Schleswig-Holstein waters. The Prussian standard was lowered at the yardarm.

"Take it away!" cried Princess Alexandra. "I will not move one step more until it is down!"

The hated flag was instantly removed.

But soon the bitterness dissolved, and all was happiness and laughter, in the joy of the family reunion in Copenhagen. There was one strange interlude which had its amusing side. The Prince and Princess of Wales visited Stockholm, leaving the baby Prince to be cared for by Queen Louise and the Christian family. This was reported back to Queen Victoria who – and not merely because of her pro-German feelings – was prepared to believe anything of the Christians.

The Queen's advisers recalled a decree of her great-great-grandfather, George II, that the Sovereign could prevent any successor to the throne from being removed from the kingdom.

Roused to anger by what she considered to be her son's irresponsibility, the Queen telegraphed demanding peremptorily that the young Prince be returned under escort to her at Balmoral. The message was never acted upon, because it was so badly mutilated in transmission that nobody could make head or tail of it!

By the time the royal party returned home the incident was forgotten. Indeed, later the Queen herself realized that there *was* something to be said for Denmark, for she became disgusted at the settlement over the Schleswig-Holstein war as a result of which Prussia gained Schleswig and Holstein went to Austria.

Meanwhile Victoria continued the mourning. The mausoleum at Frogmore was built: it is very Germanic and not attractive, but it does stand in a lovely position, and she knew that it was where her husband would have wished it to be. The grounds are quite glorious: it is very different from the crypt at St George's Chapel, which is hopelessly overcrowded, as practically all of the Royal Family down the generations seem to have been buried there.

Her people and the Dominions sympathized with the Queen, and for a while they waited, expecting Her Majesty gradually to 'come round'; but this she never really did. Her son tried to persuade her time after time, but whenever he mentioned the matter she blamed him entirely for what had happened. There was nothing he could do to help her as his father had done.

"I have my Ministers," she said whenever he broached the subject.

"But your own son could help you more personally," he protested gently.

"*I am* the Queen!"

And as Bertie once said to a friend: "What can you say to that one?"

For a decade after the Prince Consort's death the Queen would never even consider the idea – which in happier days she had proposed herself – that the Prince of Wales should "early be initiated into the affairs of State". She justified her prejudice by saying in after-years that she could "hardly bear the thought of anyone helping me, or standing where my dearest had always stood".

Meanwhile the Princess of Wales was expecting her second baby. The future King George V – christened George Frederick Ernest Albert (the last two after the Coburg brothers) – was born at Marlborough House on 3rd June 1865.

A few days later fire broke out above the nursery. The Prince of Wales showed himself to be a man of action and courage, for he hacked up the blazing floorboards and poured buckets of water on the flames to stop them spreading.

Twenty months later, on 14th February 1867, the Princess of Wales gave birth to the future Princess Royal, Princess Louise. But she became so ill with rheumatic fever that she even talked of dying and Queen Victoria came temporarily out of her glum retirement at Windsor to assure her daughter-in-law: "Darling Alix, we can't spare you!"

The fever abated, but left Alexandra with the limp which was to become famous as "the Alexandra limp".

A second daughter, Princess Victoria, whom the family called Toria, was born in July 1868: she was destined never to marry (because she was forbidden to marry a commoner whom she loved) and to be her mother's faithful companion and, after her death, her brother King George V's.

The Prince and Princess of Wales then set out on a prolonged overseas tour. There was a bit of trouble· with the Queen when they said they wanted to take their three older children – Clarence, George and Louise – to see their grandparents in Denmark. Once again the Queen protested that it was not right that the children should be taken out of the country: they must be left with her.

The Prince of Wales, who was now beginning to be talked about as another 'Prince Hal' because of the gay life he led away from home, felt it necessary to remonstrate with Mama, and in the end the Queen gave in and they set off happily for foreign parts.

The royal party went first to Paris to see Napoleon III and the Empress Eugénie, and then spent six weeks together in Denmark with Alexandra's family. The royal children were then sent home with their nannies whilst their parents went on to Berlin to see Vicky, and then to Vienna, where the Emperor Franz-Josef made a great fuss of Alexandra. After that the travellers went on to Egypt.

They spent six weeks on the Nile, the Prince shooting away at wild life to his heart's content, while Alexandra completely captured the hearts of the Egyptians by smoking a hookah and even dining with the ladies of the Khedive Ismael's harem. What Queen Victoria would have said it is impossible to think!

After a visit to Turkey – travelling incognito as "Mr and Mrs Williams" – the Prince and Princess went on to the Crimea and then finally to Greece to see Alexandra's brother the King and his Queen, Olga.

9

The Mordaunt Scandal

So ended the 1860s which had seen the failure of the Prince of Wales, because of his mother's adamant opposition, to find any useful employment in the service of the State. The 'Sixties had also seen the creation of what became known as The Marlborough House Set and its leaders – 'The Marlbocracy'.

By this time the whole world knew that the Prince of Wales loved to gamble for high stakes, to frequent the race-course, and to flirt with pretty women.

The Prince was also getting rather stout, and people behind his back called him "Tum Tum". He was then in his late twenties!

He was also a great smoker, and he had a row with the committee of White's Club in St James's when he put forward a resolution that smoking should be allowed in the morning room. The idea was turned down flat, whereupon the Prince resigned and founded a new club in Pall Mall, near Marlborough House, which was named The Marlborough and which as its founder he dominated for many years. In fact, nobody could be elected a member unless he approved the application! The Marlborough Club lasted until 1952.

By the 'Seventies it had become an unwritten rule at Marlborough House that the Princess of Wales visited her family in Denmark every autumn while Albert Edward joined the high society at the Continental spas, where he made many new friends, of whom the Queen usually disapproved. It was then that the Prince built up his long friendship with the Rothschilds, whose funds were to enable Britain, through Disraeli, to buy the Suez Canal.

At this time, too, perhaps not unnaturally, a republican movement began growing up in some of the English cities. Late in 1869 there was a mass demonstration in Hyde Park and the Prince wrote to his mother:

"I have no doubt much treason was talked ... I hear some speakers openly spoke of a Republic!"

Many of the Prince's new and fashionable friends were invited to Sandringham. The Queen warned him that *if* he became King – she did not say *when*! – he would have to break with them *all*.

The happiest times of his life were spent there and, appreciating its attractions more and more, the Prince had the house rebuilt in the grand manner which became familiar to later generations of the Royal Family.

Of course, the upper classes had looked forward to the marriage of the Prince and Princess of Wales as a new starting-point for a wider social life all round, while what they called the 'lower classes' hoped that the marriage would settle the Prince down. The unofficial 'reign' of Edward and Alexandra during Queen Victoria's voluntary isolation at Windsor – Buckingham Palace was practically closed – did in fact favour the first of these purposes.

It was a time when there were delicious scandals about the 'Upper Ten' who kept very late hours and spent fortunes living on the fat of the land, so people said, while the poor starved. In London many poor folk went barefoot, even in winter.

For the more fortunate two o'clock in the morning would have represented going 'early to bed'. The music halls were going strong and were quite delightful. They had the most diverting form of entertainment in turns, so if you did not like one the next act could be better. The Prince and his wife often went to these performances. They also liked the theatre, which was now something which most people who could afford it visited.

The Queen objected to all this high life, describing it as irresponsible and harum-scarum. She told her son so.

"I know," he told her; and in one letter to her when he was visiting Paris he informed his mother:

"Sad stories have indeed reached our ears from London of 'scandals in high life', which is indeed much to be deplored ..."

Again and again he advised his mother that if she would only return to Buckingham Palace and show herself to her people it would make all the difference in the world. She belonged here, to run the country. But the Queen firmly refused to listen.

"One can never have a reasonable argument with Mama," he complained. And that was true. Perhaps to her he was still a little boy whom she must keep suppressed.

"But, Mama, the people want to see you. They recognize you as being the Queen, and you are needed at the palace."

"I live my own life in my own way," she told him.

Sadly he told Alexandra: "I don't think she will ever come out again. If I were assassinated she wouldn't come to my funeral."

The Princess burst into tears.

"You must not say such dreadful things!" she cried.

Instantly he was all contrition. "I'm sorry. You mustn't worry. I can always put up a good fight, and God help the fellow who wants to assassinate *me*!"

He had now become almost as anti-German as Alexandra, especially after Germany had made a cold-blooded attack on her former ally, Austria, as a result of which many of Alexandra's relations were ruined.

One day when some visitor was trying to make conversation with the Princess she asked her what she would like best in the world. In a flash Alexandra answered that she would like nothing better than to see Bismarck's head on a charger.

The Princess of Wales loved her home and her children, and on 26th November 1869 the latest arrival was greeted with joy – a third daughter, Maud Charlotte Mary Victoria, who was later to become Queen Maud of Norway.

But early in 1870 one of those 'scandals' to which the Prince of Wales had made so ironical a reference in his letter to the Queen enveloped the Marlborough House Set.

One of the Prince of Wales's acquaintances was Sir Charles Mordaunt. Now Mordaunt sued his pretty, twenty-one-year-old wife for divorce, citing two of the Prince's friends as co-respondents, but they filed counter-petitions alleging that Lady Mordaunt was insane.

A subpoena was served on the Prince of Wales to appear at the hearing as a witness, as he had written the lady several letters and had also visited her.

The Prince protested his innocence not only to his friends and advisers but also to his wife – and his mother!

Lady Mordaunt had known the Prince since she had made her curtsy to him when she was presented at Court. She was a gay, cheerful girl when she was launched upon her exciting 'season' as a debutante. Her parents happened to be neighbours of the Queen's at Balmoral, and before the girl 'came out' in London she had gone to one or two parties at Marlborough House at the invitation of the Prince and Princess of Wales.

Soon after she had entered Society and completed her season she married Mordaunt, a rather serious-minded older man, the sort of man one would not have expected her to choose, but he was rich, and maybe she was under pressure from home. Afterwards she went from party to party – and then the divorce scandal broke.

The Prince of Wales was utterly horrified!

When this very pretty young Lady Mordaunt had married she had cut down her social engagements in accordance with her husband's wishes. He did not approve of too much gaiety. She was not accustomed to being given orders, nor was she a clever girl, and she missed her good times. She was used to having fun, and she saw no reason to sweep aside her friendship with the Prince of Wales (which naturally made her very proud), and she did not obey her husband's orders to the letter.

When her little daughter was born, for some reason her suspicious husband changed his tune and became wildly jealous. He thought that the child was not his, though he had no reason in the world to think so. He declared that she had been unfaithful. Then the papers got hold of the news and various stories went the rounds, as they usually do in such cases.

This was one of the greatest shocks that the country had had probably since the attempted divorce of Queen Caroline by George IV.

One cannot imagine what the Prince felt about it when the ghastly news was broken to him. The chatter had buzzed through London soon after this poor girl's baby had been born – and born blind, it seemed, which must have been a terrible shock to her.

While his wife was lying-in her husband searched her papers and found a valentine sent to her by the Prince of Wales, among other correspondence. The girl had to admit that the Prince had been writing to her.

The case aroused widespread interest. Most loyal subjects said "It can't be true!" but others averred that "they had always known that something funny was going on; he was always here, there and everywhere".

Outwardly the Queen was surprisingly controlled and reasonable. The Prince appeared to have been cheered by her and to be happier after he had seen her.

He declined to claim privilege and elected to be examined in the witness-box, something which everybody thought he might get out of somehow, but there is no playing with a court of law. He must have been chilled with horror at the prospect, but the Princess of Wales took it nobly, going on with her engagements, not retiring from public view, as some said she would, while the case was hanging over them. She was the most remarkable woman in the way she adored him, and she helped him greatly behind the scenes. Yet inwardly she felt humiliated and distressed. So did those ladies, not least the Duchess of Cambridge and her daughter, who had helped to bring Bertie and Alix together in the first place.

There was a tremendous thrill about the case, with crowds of people queueing for hours to try to get seats in court. Serjeant Ballantyne appeared on behalf of Sir Charles Mordaunt and made no attempt to ease things for the unfortunate Prince of Wales: in fact, he tried to involve him further. The whole atmosphere of the crowded court (with mobs of people waiting outside) tended to make the Prince's ordeal considerably worse.

There was the evidence of the lady's maid and of the butler – both faithful servants of the Mordaunts – who told the court that the Prince of Wales called on Lady Mordaunt when she was alone and always in the late afternoon. In those days the late afternoon was a popular time for paying visits. The servants were given very normal directions that nobody else was to be admitted while the Prince was there. This was usual with royal visitors; no outsiders came in.

There seemed very little in it, but the Prince was part of the gay life of London. This did not help him. In this world there are always people who insist that there is 'no smoke without fire'.

It was the most ghastly plight for the heir to the throne to find himself in, but he did have one wonderful stroke of luck. A provincial newspaper had managed to get hold of copies of some of his letters to the girl involved, and these they contrived to print. There was not a sign of any love affair in them. He had known Lady Mordaunt since she was a schoolgirl, was interested in her career, worried about her unhappy marriage, and there was no suggestion of any sort that he had been in love with her. Lord Hatherley, the Lord Chancellor, wrote that the issue of a subpoena was "extraordinary" in view of the trifling nature of these letters.

The Prince was in the witness-box for only seven minutes. He was examined by Lady Mordaunt's counsel, Dr Deane. He denied that he had committed adultery. He spoke coolly and was not in the least embarrassed, although he must have been in a furious temper at finding himself in such a stupid position. He was not, after all, cross-examined by Serjeant Ballantyne, the claimant's counsel.

Mordaunt's claim failed at that time on the grounds that his wife was prevented by insanity from being a party to the suit.

It was the saddest aspect of this affair that the poor young girl concerned actually went out of her mind and died in a madhouse very soon afterwards.

The Queen was relieved that the Prince of Wales had come out of an awkward situation with a certain amount of dignity, and she agreeably surprised her son by sending him a letter of congratulation. But she had earlier warned the Lord Chancellor that the case could injure the Prince in the eyes of the "middle and lower classes", which was most deeply to be lamented in those days when "the higher classes in their frivolous, selfish and pleasure-seeking lives, do more to increase the spirit of democracy than anything else". Democracy then had a different meaning from its meaning today: the word was not used without a shudder in polite society.

Although the Prince was virtually cleared, the public did not accept the result of the case in the way he would have expected. He and the Princess of Wales were hissed in the streets of London. They were booed when they entered the royal box at the Olympic Theatre. But boos at Ascot in that year of 1870 turned to cheers when a horse in which the Prince had some interest won a race, and he commented that the crowd seemed to be in a better temper with him when he left the course than they had been when he arrived.

He thought that when he had left the court, cleared, he had restored the nation's confidence in him because he was declared innocent, and I am perfectly sure that he *was* innocent. But he realized immediately that all this scandal was going to take some living down, for some people were only too ready to jump at the idea that there was something odd happening and to make the most of it. He was surprised to find that his mother was on his side – outwardly, at least – and was absolutely furious with people for behaving so badly towards him.

In those days the mere mention of divorce was highly scandalous, and he supposed that the opinion of the world was that he must have done something scandalous to get himself mixed up in it! It was not discussed in respectable houses, being considered utterly shocking, and for a Prince to do it, too! He was hissed yet again when he went to the Crystal Palace with the Princess.

That was too much.

From the very beginning the Princess of Wales had been on her husband's side, and she remained this way. She had always known that women appealed to her husband, and she had been kindly lenient to him about it. Naturally there were newspapers who boosted their sales by making the most of his affairs of the heart, but there were also some who defended the Prince most gallantly. He was most amazed that his mother could be so tolerant, for tolerance was not her strong suit. She was indeed a curious woman.

Once again he seized the opportunity to ask her for a job abroad, the post he had always wanted, but she said (and in a way this was true) that it would seem as if he were trying to run away from all the talk, and that would do nobody any good at all. But she *was* sympathetic, and that was something.

She told him that the best thing to do would be to give up frivolous company – to go on living as usual at Marlborough House but with perhaps fewer late-night parties. For a time he abided by her advice, and was astonished that she was so amiable about it.

There was, however, no gainsaying the fact that the Princess of Wales was deeply hurt by the Mordaunt affair. She was the most sweetly tolerant woman and never jealous. She believed in her husband, for in Denmark she had been told that all Englishmen were flirtatious, they flirted gaily and did not mean anything by it.

Whether she accepted that as the truth I am not sure, for it could at times have been difficult for her, but the Princess adored Bertie and never complained.

"When we come to the throne there will be no time for fun," he told her – so he took it whilst he had the chance.

Alexandra was also devoted to her children and kept them at home with her as much as she could. "A royal court," she said, "is not the right place for children."

All this time, however, she and her husband were having trouble with the Queen. The Government put up suggestions for Victoria to make a gradual return to Buckingham Palace, but whenever the idea was proposed she blankly refused to entertain it.

She saw the family fairly often, and she loved her grandchildren; but gradually the truth dawned on Bertie and Alix that the Queen never intended to live *as the Queen* again, although she retained the title, never dreamt of abdicating, and expected to be consulted about everything.

She was intensely obstinate, of course – one of those people whom you could never persuade to take any action and, as her son said, nobody in this world could ever talk Mama around!

"This is going on for ever," Edward told a friend in confidence. "I shall grow old and die without ever having been allowed to do a single thing for my country, and Mama will live for ever!"

It did look rather like it.

His mother's stubbornness was one of the reasons why the Prince of Wales sought company outside his home. Another was Princess Alexandra's deep sense of motherhood: she was very home-keeping, loved the domestic scene more than most of her predecessors, and was very boastful about her children. Altogether she had six children, three boys and three girls, but the youngest boy died in infancy. The three daughters were so overwhelmed by the beauty and the dominating personality of their lovely mother that they scarcely spoke in company or, if they did, they communicated in whispers. They were known as "Their Royal Shynesses" and, in Court circles, as "the whispering Wales sisters".

The Prince of Wales was thoroughly bored. The Princess of Wales must have known how much he fretted at times, for she realized that there was so much that he wanted to do for his country, to ensure permanent peace, but all the time he was hindered by the Queen, to whom he complained: "This is a sheer waste of living."

Victoria ignored all this. She could be extremely unpleasant when she wished; it had been something that her husband had been able to control, but their son could not! She wanted to keep her queenship to herself – the Widow at Windsor, as she became – and there was nothing that he could do to change her.

"I have never been her favourite son," he said with a wry smile – and this was true.

He thought he could do good work in the Colonies, but she would permit nothing of the sort. However, she did one thing that surprised him. She said that she would go up to London to lay the foundation stone of the Royal Albert Hall, built to the memory of the Prince Consort.

Nobody had ever thought that she would do so, but she did. If the nation thought that this would mean that she would return to public life they were wrong. The Prince of Wales wrote to a sister:

My royal mother is going to lay the foundation stone of the Royal Albert Hall, which is to be built in memory of our father. I wish she would perform her duty to the living as she does to the dead!

It was fair comment. The Queen lived in the past. Whenever a new Governor was wanted for one of the Colonies, or something of that sort cropped up, the Prince of Wales went and asked his mother about it, but she always found some excuse for not giving him the job.

It was all very depressing and frustrating.

10
The Gay Life

All the while the Prince of Wales was moving more and more in a gay circle of friends, of whom his mother more and more severely disapproved.

After the Mordaunt affair the Princess of Wales departed for Denmark. This time it seemed as though their separation was a serious one, but it was cut short by the outbreak of the Franco-Prussian War. The Queen thought the Prussians might invade Denmark, and she ordered Alexandra to return post-haste. The Prince of Wales travelled to Copenhagen to bring her home, and there was a great reconciliation.

When the Franco-Prussian War was being fought a lot of people said that Edward was pro-German. The contrary was the truth. He still adored France and hoped that the Germans would get thoroughly and soundly beaten.

The war ended with one of those Prussian peace pacts in which Germany got everything – including her empire – that she could out of France. The Prince had never trusted Bismarck, who at once reminded him that as his father had been a German he had no right to talk against Germany.

The Prince stuck to his guns. There was some disturbance when he went to dine with the Prussian ambassador, Count von Bernstorff, where apparently the Prince said, "Never trust a German!"

This remark came from the heart. News of it went the rounds and was picked up by his sister, the Princess Royal, who wrote to Mama about it. It was the sort of thing that one says on the spur of the moment (usually the Prince was more

Four generations: Queen
Victoria, the future
Edward VII, George V
and Edward VIII

Edward VII at
Sandringham, mounted
on his favourite pony

Queen Alexandra in her coronation robes, 22nd January 1901

discreet), but the Queen was furious and sent for him to explain. Was not her late husband a German, and her son also?

There followed one of those formidable rows at which the Queen was particularly adept! It had been an absurd thing for the son of a German prince to say. He told her then how much he hated war, and how it disgusted him that the Germans were so fond of martial glory. She replied that all nations can make mistakes. But he would not apologize, and afterwards in a letter to his mother he wrote:

"The truth is that I cannot bear sitting here and doing nothing whilst all this blood-letting is going on."

He suggested that he himself should go and see the King of Prussia – the Emperor of Germany as he soon became – in the hopes of getting an armistice *pro tem* which perhaps could become the corner-stone of a wider peace.

The Queen was not the sort of woman to be advised by her son, and she said so. She used the opportunity to hark back on that "disgraceful divorce". She could never let well alone.

So the unhappy Prince went from one house party to another, from one race meeting to another, gaming, gambling, shooting, playing tennis, and philandering with pretty women.

Among his best friends was Henry (Viscount) Chaplin, son-in-law of the Duke of Sutherland: he was well versed in fast horses and in equally go-ahead young women! Lord Houston and the sixth Marquess of Waterford and his younger brother Charles Beresford were also great friends: all enjoyed living the good life.

The Prince realized, as he said to one of them, "When I come to the throne I shall never have the time for this sort of thing, so I had better make hay whilst the sun shines!"

He had forgotten the Mordaunt Case and was inclined to ignore the warning once the danger was past. He was frequently to be seen at gambling clubs and fashionable country houses ogling coquettish women. 'Skittles', the famous Catherine Walters, inveigled him to tea parties with some of her beautiful friends and introduced him to baccarat parties at her Mayfair clubs. He went a few times to Cremorne Gardens and was often at Evans' Music Hall in Covent Garden, where he was carefully screened from the public gaze: his mother had warned him to be careful!

For Alexandra the times were not so good. The death of her last baby and the terrible heartache of the Mordaunt Case were now followed by fearful anxiety over the Heir to the Throne himself. The Prince of Wales contracted typhoid, that dread disease which had stricken down his father.

In November 1871 he was at death's door. The Queen and the Royal Family gathered around his bedside at Sandringham and prayed hard. Their prayers were answered. A few days before the "awful anniversary" (14th December) of the Prince Consort's death the Queen was advised that there was no hope for her son.

Miraculously he improved that same night. The crisis passed. In her frantic prayers the Queen spoke of "my beloved child"!

The Prince slowly recovered, and his biographer has recorded that the fact of his recovery "destroyed republicanism overnight as a significant factor in British radical politics".

Thirteen thousand people invaded St Paul's Cathedral and its precincts for a memorial thanksgiving service. *The Lancet* reported that one spectator gaped so much at the size of the crowd that he dislocated his jaw and had to receive medical attention.

Now the Prince of Wales regained his lost popularity, which was to last most of his life. He was for a time even popular with his mother, and Mr Gladstone used the better atmosphere at Windsor to pursue an earlier proposal of Mr Disraeli that the Prince of Wales should be appointed her representative in Ireland. Another plan was that the Prince and his household should transfer from Marlborough House to Buckingham Palace.

The Queen would not hear of either project.

Well-meaning ministers thought that the Prince should in some way improve his mind, and Gladstone – himself a scholar – was bold enough to ask the Queen to try to persuade her son to "adopt the habit of reading".

But the Queen well knew that Bertie had never been fond of reading anything substantial, although he was an expert on the sporting papers and racing form.

"From his earliest years," she said, "it was *impossible* to get him to do so. Newspapers and, *very rarely*, a novel, are all he ever reads."

In France, after the defeat of Napoleon III, another republic had taken over and the exiled Emperor and his Empress, Eugénie, fled to England, to be welcomed most cordially by the Prince of Wales and his wife. The rulers of this Third Republic seemed to be extremely hostile because England had accepted them as their guests, but the Prince defended them stoutly!

When Napoleon died in January 1873 the Queen gave her permission for her son to attend his funeral at Chislehurst. But Gladstone asked him to stay away, at which the Prince made it clear to everyone that he would not only attend but would go further: he invited to Sandringham a number of Bonapartists who had sailed across the Channel to make a public demonstration against the Third Republic as well as against their Emperor's hated enemy, the Germans.

Alexandra's deafness was increasing at this time. Her doctors could do nothing about it. She became ever more attached to her home while her husband went more or less his own way. But she never allowed his infidelities to undermine their home life, their loving relations with their children, or their mutual respect.

Life became gayer. While Alexandra visited Denmark, the Prince preferred the waters at Baden. He also, like his predecessor, George IV, piled up colossal debts. In the early 'Seventies these were said to have reached £600,000. This, of course, was nothing to be compared to the commitments of his mother's detested uncle!

By this time Prince Eddy (Clarence) and Prince George had been launched on naval careers as cadets, though the elder boy to his grandmother's disappointment was deficient in many ways and he never stuck at it as his brother did.

Their mother very much wanted to accompany their father on a tour of India in the mid-'Seventies, as she believed it her duty to be with the Prince of Wales rather than with her children on such occasions. This, it is not without interest to note, was the view taken by Queen Alexandra's daughter-in-law, the future Queen Mary, in her time. (Queen Victoria absolutely refused to let Alexandra leave her children, but when he became King the Prince of Wales was only too pleased to see *his* daughter-in-law accompany George on visits abroad!)

"I have had great tiger shooting," the Prince of Wales wrote to Eddy and George. "The day before yesterday I killed six."

The tour was a brilliant success politically, but it was marred by a scandal at home as a result of which the Prince and one of his friends, Lord Randolph Churchill, were estranged.

On his return the Prince again took up with his mother the vexed problem of how he was to be employed in the service of the State. Nothing happened. Meanwhile he dallied with some of the famous beauties of the day, including Lillie Langtry – the fabulous 'Jersey Lily'. When Lillie rode with the future King in Rotten Row people scuffled to get a better look at her.

On top of her deafness Alexandra at this time tended to become more unpunctual than ever. Because of her deafness she could not enjoy those pleasures which were so much a part of her husband's life, and her unpunctuality enraged him more and more.

She was sad about these shortcomings of hers and made no excuse for them, but she never lacked friends, among them Mr and Mrs Gladstone (indeed, the Prime Minister, the scourge of Queen Victoria, who regarded him as a 'firebrand', was grateful to the Princess for her friendship), and she could depend also on courtiers such as Oliver Montagu, who served her faithfully and chivalrously until his untimely death in 1893.

Queen Victoria knew about her son's affairs, of course, and frankly told him that it was a disgrace. It was no use his telling her that if she would only give him something useful to do she might have less to complain about in this direction.

His frustration reached boiling-point in the summer of 1882 when Gladstone ordered the bombardment of Alexandria and the dispatch of a British army to invade and occupy Egypt. Very much the same sort of situation developed – but with more success – as was to follow the Suez 'war' of 1956.

The Prince of Wales made "a gallant effort" to join the Egyptian expedition, begging the Queen to let him serve in any capacity with the Guards.

His anxiety could be the better understood when it is recalled that at this time he was a field marshal and that he was taunted by the Germans – and even by some Frenchmen – because his experience had so far been limited to the annual "battle of flowers" on the Riviera. And Bismarck despicably and untruthfully alleged that his love of uniforms was matched only by his fear of gunpowder.

The Queen "finally and conclusively" decided that the Prince could not accompany the British force either as a participant or as a spectator (observer).

A by-product of this disappointment was that the Prince took up lawn tennis, which had been introduced to the country a few years earlier. He played this game, as he fenced, largely in an effort to cut down his weight, but in the process he acquired some skill: his example inspired others to take up tennis and raised the game to world eminence.

Now he was having trouble with that old bogy of his, the son of his eldest sister – Prince Wilhelm who would later become Kaiser of Germany.

From the very first time they had met they had disliked each other very much indeed. The Prince of Wales found Willy a most obstinate, trying little boy, though he knew that the Queen adored him: she might not have retained this affection for her first-born grandchild had she lived long enough to see what he did.

In the autumn of 1880 the future Emperor had become engaged to the daughter of the Duke of Augustenberg: she was known at Court as "Dona".

Feeling very grown-up, Willy – encouraged by Bismarck – began to treat his mother shamefully. Bismarck and other courtiers called her "the Englishwoman", and Bismarck told her son she was trying to run Germany on the orders of her mother, Queen Victoria, and the uncle whom he had now grown to despise. Nevertheless, the Prince of Wales, largely to keep the peace on the domestic front and also to please his mother, attended Willy's wedding in February of the following year. Alexandra did not.

Tragedy struck the Royal Family a month later. Alexander II, father-in-law of Alexandra's sister Dagmar, was assassinated by a bomb after he had reviewed troops in St Petersburg. The Queen forbade her son to attend the funeral, but the Prince of Wales and his wife reassured her, and they sailed for Russia.

They found the atmosphere in St Petersburg very sinister and even menacing, and they were warned by the police chief that their safety could be guaranteed only if they stayed away from the new Czar Alexander III and his Czarina, as Alexandra's sister had become.

Even the Czar and his wife were isolated, and when the British royals went to the Crimea to relax with their relations their villa had to be guarded by a large police force.

Of course, during this meeting there was much criticism of Willy and the Prussian Court. When the Prince of Wales visited Berlin for his sister's silver wedding celebrations Willy had become quite impossible and was strutting around in Royal Stuart tartan, sent to him by his adoring grandmother at Windsor.

The Prince of Wales was sick to death of doing nothing and being subjected to the sneers of his revolting nephew Willy. He was a modern-minded man who saw the faults behind many of the old rules and regulations and conventions. He said that this was no time to be standing around doing nothing!

He was therefore glad when in 1884 he was invited to serve on a Royal Commission on the Housing of the Working Classes. Other members included his friend, Lord Carrington, and Cardinal Manning and the Marquess of Salisbury.

At Lord Carrington's suggestion the Prince welcomed a chance to visit – in disguise – some of the worst slums in Clerkenwell and St Pancras and Holborn, those noisome backwaters of Victorian London. The Prince was horrified by what he saw, and a few days later, in the House of Lords, he made a blistering attack on the Government for its failure to improve housing conditions.

His work on the Commission was interrupted by the death of his haemophiliac brother Leopold at Cannes, and once again, just when it seemed that the Queen might emerge from her shell, the Court was plunged into ever-deeper mourning.

The hope that the Prince of Wales might be able to get away from home to do some useful work abroad was revived when in the late summer of 1884 an expeditionary force was recruited to go to the relief of General Gordon at Khartoum. Once again the Prince strongly urged the Queen to let him sail with it, but permission was again withheld; and the Prince was indeed engaged in the "battle of flowers" at Cannes when he heard early in 1885 that Khartoum had fallen and that Gordon had been slain before the relief expedition could reach the Sudanese capital.

Later the same year the Prince, who had always yearned to be able to do something to solve the Irish problem, toured Ireland with Princess Alexandra and Prince Eddy. This was their second State visit to that unhappy country in seven years, during which time there had been the terrible Phoenix Park murders when Lord Frederick Cavendish and Mr Burke were assassinated by terrorists.

Now the Fenians had placed a price of £2,000 on the head of the Prince of Wales. It was to show his contempt for them and their trifling 'blood money' that the Prince brushed aside all objections and went to Ireland. Bombs were dropped everywhere. Edward pooh-poohed them. He kept his police escort to a minimum so that he could see the people and the people could see him – and especially see the Princess, whose wonderful smile and genuine sympathy with the lot of the poor did much to calm down an otherwise threatening situation.

After this triumph came the greater – and immortal – triumph of Queen Victoria's Jubilee in 1887. The Prince sent his wife to Windsor to discuss with the Queen a suggestion that she might wear State robes at Westminster Abbey. It was cast aside indignantly! The Queen resolutely refused to exchange her eternal mourning dress for something more appropriate to the spirit of national rejoicing at the fact that she had reigned over the British people for fifty glorious years.

The 1880s ended on a sour royal note. The old Emperor Wilhelm I of Germany died in March 1888: his death coincided with the silver wedding of the Prince and Princess of Wales.

Alexandra refused to attend the old man's funeral, referring to him as "the thief who stole Schleswig-Holstein".

The German imperial throne now passed to Albert Edward's handsome but ailing brother-in-law Fritz, who became the Emperor Frederick III. But he was already in the grip of throat cancer. His last days were made the more agonizing by the cruel behaviour of his son Willy, especially towards his desperately sad mother.

The Emperor died after a very brief reign and Willy succeeded him as Wilhelm II (and last). Alexandra agreed to attend the funeral, which meant visiting hated Germany, largely for the sake of Vicky, the bereaved Empress. She returned to London declaring, "Willy is *mad*!"

By 1890 the new young Emperor was abusing his uncle as

"the old Peacock", but Queen Victoria made Willy an honorary Admiral of the Fleet and as he arrived at Cowes in his flashy yacht, the *Hohenzollern*, he nudged his uncle and said: "Fancy wearing the same uniform as Nelson!"

The Emperor further mortified his uncle by remarking that he was "the only Crown Prince in Europe who has not seen active service".

It was little wonder that some observers of the royal scene in those days, as the "naughty 'Nineties" got under way, foresaw the bitterness which was developing between the Kaiser and the future King Edward VII as a potential source of trouble which could alter the course of world history.

11

Tranby Croft

Over the years the Prince of Wales had run heavily into debt. Not only was he extravagant, but he also led the life of a country gentleman, no expenses spared, and his outlay on horse-racing and his gambling and other adventures made it impossible for him to live within his income – though he was never in the same class as George IV as a big spender.

His debts escalated. As a young man of twenty-four, for instance, he had become used to losing small sums at cards, but in one night he was £138 down – a lot of money in those days – after playing eight rubbers of whist with people like Sir Robert Peel and the Duke of St Albans.

A year later he lost as much as £300 or £400 at a single sitting at White's Club.

He was also betting fairly heavily, for he enjoyed this. He took risks on the Turf which meant that he lost very often. His mother's purse was closed to him, and he had to turn to others for the wherewithal. Thus he wrote to Charles Carrington:

As you probably will not be back in time to settle my account at Tattersall's, do you mind writing or telegraphing to some friends to do so in *your* name?

Our account is – I win £300 on *Vauban* – lose £100 on *Plaudit* – and win £75 on *Plaudit* – making a total of £275, I win. This is, I hope, correct. At any rate I have put it in my book ... Remember me to those wicked boys, Blandford and Oliver.

Betting had always given him a tremendous thrill, but he was not very lucky at it, and he had to admit this. Whatever happened, he could never turn to Mama for, although she was very rich, she would never spend a halfpenny more than she could help. She had worn the same old dress for years and she detested the idea of any member of her family ever getting into debt, even more if he was one of her sons.

Shooting and yachting also exercised a growing fascination for the Prince over the years, but horse-racing and card-playing vied for his favour with flirting with and chasing pretty women.

Baccarat was the craze of the hour, and in the last decade of the Queen's reign it got Edward into more trouble. The game was illegal, although it was allowed to be played in private houses. At Sandringham it was played nearly every night when the Prince was in residence. According to one guest, "They have a real table, and rakes, and everything like the rooms at Monte Carlo!"

During the St Leger week the Prince usually stayed with his friend Christopher Sykes, but by the September of 1890 things were going badly for Sykes: he faced bankruptcy and could scarcely act as host to the rather expensive Heir to the Throne.

Instead he went with the Prince to stay at Tranby Croft, near Doncaster. As things turned out, it was an unfortunate choice. Tranby Croft was the home of a shipowner, Arthur Wilson. This was the first time the Prince had ever been to Tranby Croft, so he did not know much about his host. As usual on such occasions, he took with him his personal set of counters, each engraved with the plumes of the Prince of Wales's badge.

At this time the Society beauty most in the Prince's favour was Lady Brooke, who was to become the radiant Countess of Warwick and the Prince's "darling Daisy". Lord Warwick seems to have played very little part in the love story of his beautiful countess and the future King, but he did once flare up about it.

Edward had sent Lady Warwick the most extravagant gift of a glorious carriage and a pair of grey horses to go with it. I think it must have arrived at a bad moment in the earl's life, for apparently he flew into a rage. He himself shot both horses and then had the carriage hacked to pieces. There is no story of what her ladyship said about it, nor, if it comes to that, what her royal lover said when he knew. It could have been the beginning of the end!

However, at the time of the Tranby Croft affair these were early days in the love story of the Prince and the Countess (as she became in 1893). "Daisy" was the best-looking of three exquisite sisters. Edward later used to go down to Warwick Castle in one of the new-fangled "horseless carriages" which everybody then said would never catch on because they were wildly unsafe. People wondered why the Prince of Wales was allowed to risk himself in one of them.

In the ordinary way the future countess would have been with the Prince at Tranby Croft. Perhaps it was a good thing that she was not, otherwise the resultant scandal might have been worse.

On the first night of the Prince's visit, as the guests sat around the baccarat table, Arthur Wilson, junior, the shipowner's son, saw one of the party cheating! He was Sir William Gordon-Cumming, a baronet and a lieutenant-colonel in the Scots Guards. He took one extra card, getting rid of one that was not so helpful: he did this twice.

Wilson, senior, did not know what to do, so he consulted the Prince of Wales, who felt bound to take action – a great pity, for he hoped that privately the whole unfortunate affair could be smoothed over. The Prince was still trying to live down the memory of that wretched divorce case, and rather naturally he did not want to have a great card-cheating scandal to go with it! The world is only too ready to blame others and far too slow to forgive (perhaps it never forgets), and he wanted to keep quiet.

The one idea was to avoid scandal and manage this affair between themselves. Of course, Gordon-Cumming – who had won more than £200 during the two evenings when he was detected cheating – denied the accusation, especially as most of the money was won from the 'banker', the Prince of Wales! But in the end he was made to confess, and he gave his word in writing that he would never touch a card again. Provided that he did so none of his companions would divulge what had happened. Far better to forget the whole thing! So it was agreed. The Prince witnessed the document – a profound mistake – as did the others, and had it locked away among his private papers.

If they thought that they could manage things as easily as this they were mistaken, for the secret leaked out and the next thing the Prince heard was that Gordon-Cumming planned to sue his five original accusers (not, of course, the Prince, who had been more than kind to him).

Every attempt was made to hush up the scandal, especially to avoid the necessity for the Prince – once again – to stand in the witness-box in a court of law and be cross-examined.

But by the time the case came on before Lord Chief Justice Coleridge the following year the Prince was sick with worry because most people by this time thought that *he* was the one who had been caught cheating at cards, whereas it was through his own good nature, as one of his family said, that he had been ensnared. In his vulnerable position it is not surprising that he was subpoenaed as a witness for the prosecution.

The trouble was, of course, as I have said, that baccarat was illegal in Britain, and Gordon-Cumming's counsel made the most of his opportunities to accuse the Prince of Wales of conniving at law-breaking and of trying to victimize the plaintiff in order to save his honour as the royal sponsor of an illegal game of cards.

Although the Queen at first was very understanding, when the newspapers began to fill up with details of "this horrible Trial", as she called it, she burst into protest, saying it was "a terrible humiliation ... very painful ... must do his prestige great harm ... " – very much the same words as she had used during the Mordaunt affair. One must admit that, charming man as the Prince could be, he was extremely indiscreet at times.

The case was heard at the end of the 'Season' and lasted

several days, on most of which the Prince sat uncomfortably in
court. But after consulting in private for only about twelve
minutes the jury found in favour of the defendants and against
Gordon-Cumming.

Not only did Gordon-Cumming lose his case, but he was
also dismissed the Army, expelled from all his clubs, and
socially ruined. The Prince of Wales and his friends could not
find a good thing to say of him.

But the Queen was furious by this time. The Prince, by
contrast, took it all very calmly, but his mother could not
overlook the fact that the newspapers had bandied about the
names of royal personages who could not reply to the
monstrous charges made against them. Yet nothing would
have made her believe that this was not "Bertie's fault" and,
as she said, "It is so much worse when one is growing old."

As the Prince of Wales and his wife faced yet another –
though momentary – burst of unpopularity, the Queen
pointed out to her daughter Vicky that if Bertie, having been
"dragged through the dirt", was "lowered and despised" by
the people the monarchy was itself put in danger. It was true,
of course.

What made things worse was that the frightful Willy wrote
the Queen an unctuous letter from Berlin saying how wrong it
was for his uncle to become involved in a card-sharping
scandal while he held the honorary rank of a colonel in the
Prussian Hussars!

The old Queen was retreating more and more into her shell.
Her son made an attempt to get her to stand back and let him
take over so that she might quietly enjoy her old age. I have
always felt that many of the social difficulties in which the
Prince found himself embroiled had been more her fault than
his. She would never let him help her a single inch of the way.
He saw her do the wrong things and the country grow tired of
her! The nation needed leadership, a strong leader, and here
he was standing by, unable to do anything.

His family had grown up. Prince Eddy would follow his

father on the throne one day, Prince George had survived an almost fatal attack of typhoid and remained utterly devoted to the Navy.

There had been much discussion about whom the Duke of Clarence should marry, and ultimately his engagement was announced to Princess Mary (May) of Teck, the only daughter of the Duke of Teck and his wife Princess Mary Adelaide, a granddaughter of King George III, so Hanoverian blood flowed through the veins of both young people.

A wedding befitting a future King was, of course, a costly business. The Tecks were living well beyond their means, and more or less as pensioners of the Queen, at the White Lodge in Richmond Park, of which the Prince of Wales had so many mixed memories! They were hard up, a fact which the Queen had recognized more than once in their lives, but once again she came to their rescue. On such family occasions she could be both generous and helpful.

Queen Victoria was particularly partial to the bride-to-be. She summoned May and one of her brothers to Balmoral so that she could judge the girl at first hand. She found May to be a superior kind of girl and also "very pretty". A few weeks later May and her family happened to be in the Malvern Hills and visited Worcester Cathedral, where in a casual tour of its treasures she saw the tomb of Prince Arthur, the elder brother of King Henry VIII. It made no impression on her at the time, but she remembered it in the light of later events.

The Duke of Clarence proposed to May at Luton Hoo at the end of 1891. The wedding was arranged for 27th February 1892. The young Princess spent the Christmas of 1891 with her future in-laws and her fiancé at Sandringham. A large house party had been planned to celebrate the young Duke's twenty-eighth birthday in the New Year, but meanwhile a lot of people had gone down under influenza in one of the worst epidemics ever recorded.

Princess May found Prince Eddy quite unwell. He had never been strong, and had had a bad cold, which had worsened because, getting sick of bed, he had got up and gone shooting during the Christmas week. The weather was mild at the time, but too cold for him, and he returned home feeling worse. Two great doctors travelled down from London to see him, but nothing could be done. The young girl was horrified to see his condition worsening, and she stood behind the Princess of Wales, who held her eldest son in her arms, where he died. The girl who was to have been his bride had never seen death before, and it must have been ghastly for her.

The family tried to comfort her; she always said that they were goodness itself, especially the Prince of Wales, and the dead Prince's younger brother, who was horrified, for he was devoted to the Royal Navy, and now knew that one day he would have to leave the Senior Service in order to be King.

Nobody had even thought of the possibility of this, and Princess May returned to the White Lodge in the deepest mourning. She knew that an entire trousseau which she believed now she would never need, was locked away there for her. For the moment she was broken-hearted!

His father said afterwards that, although it had seemed too terrible when it happened, it was the best possible thing for his second son (by far the more reliable of the two Princes), for George and Princess May shared their grief, and in the end this brought them very close, and they became engaged.

In 1893 they were married at the Chapel Royal in St James's Palace: the Queen made no objection as she had on the occasion of the marriage of Edward and Alexandra. The Prince of Wales was delighted for them, although Alexandra, who in the family was known as "darling Motherdear", was not too anxious to lose her "darling Georgie boy" to another woman! The Prince gave them York Cottage at Sandringham as their married home. It was the sharing of a common grief that had brought them close to one another (although there is some evidence that May had not been deeply in love with Prince Eddy), and theirs turned out to be a very happy marriage. The old Queen was enchanted, and was delighted when their first son arrived at the White Lodge, where the

Edward VII in coronation robes

King Edward and Queen Alexandra on the royal yacht at Cowes
in 1909

Duchess of Teck had insisted that her precious daughter – her "chick", as she called her – should lie in during the very hot summer of 1894.

That summer the Queen seems to have been surprisingly well, for she travelled by special train from Windsor to Richmond and drove to the park to visit "dear May and the darling Baby" and to choose his names. She had a genius for name-choosing, and for her great-grandson selected Albert Edward Christian George Andrew Patrick David. In the family circle the future Duke of Windsor was always to be known as David.

The new century dawned, and there were four children at York Cottage – three boys and the only girl, Mary, her father's joy.

In April 1900 the Prince and Princess of Wales paid yet another visit to Copenhagen. This time they went first to Belgium. Their train stopped for an exchange of courtesies at Brussels, and while they were waiting at the station for their train to move off a revolver was poked through the window of their carriage at them.

The gunman, an anarchist named Sipido, only fifteen years old, fired point-blank at the Prince. The bullet missed. Miss Charlotte Knollys, the Princess's lady-in-waiting and confidante, felt a sharp twinge as the bullet pierced her bun and embedded itself behind her head in the upholstery.

"No harm done," reported the Prince of Wales. "The Princess is none the worse and bore everything with the greatest courage and fortitude."

He urged that Sipido was too young to know what he was doing, and asked the authorities to deal with him as leniently as possible. The boy was afterwards freed under police supervision until he came of age. The Prince had not intended that he should be treated *that* leniently, and he was rather put out.

Meanwhile he asked for the bullet which had so nearly

ended his life. He then put it in an envelope which he marked "Sipido's bullet, Brussels, April 1900" and had it put away in the archives at Windsor Castle.

The Boer War had by this time involved Britain in difficulties overseas, and, as is well-known, Kaiser Wilhelm II took advantage of them to advance his own cause. But it is perhaps useful to record, in the light of after-events, that instead of going to France for the Easter holidays in 1900 the Prince of Wales had made the trip to Denmark because of the anti-British hostility of the French newspapers. Yet the *Entente Cordiale* was not far off.

The Queen was dying. After the Diamond Jubilee in 1897 she had begun to fade. But her dynasty – unlike that of the Hanoverians – was securely founded. There were already the four great-grandchildren at York Cottage – three sons as well as Mary, with the possibility of more children on the way – when in January 1901 there came news that Victoria's life was flickering.

As he approached the end of his fifth decade the Prince of Wales had, by this time, made many new friends and discarded some of the old ones. Sir Ernest Cassel had replaced those who, like Baron Hirsch, had advised him in financial matters.

By 1898 Lady Warwick had gone out of his life – she became a socialist – and her place had been taken by Mrs George Keppel, then twenty-nine, whose good looks, cleverness and vivacity endeared her to the Court and whose influence on Edward, especially after he became King, was benign and useful. Alice Keppel was the daughter of an admiral and the wife of a brother of Lord Albemarle.

Another family friendship burgeoned with that lady who became famous to later generations as "Sister Agnes". She was Miss Agnes Keyser, who with the help of the King and his friends founded a military officers' nursing home later known as King Edward's Hospital for Officers.

The scene was now set for the new reign. For some years the Prince of Wales had been "killing time", as he called it, when he suddenly became aware that his mother's long reign was about to pass into history.

She died at Osborne in the evening of 22nd January 1901. She had been on the throne for nearly sixty-four years.

As soon as it was known that she was dying her dutiful grandson, Wilhelm II, rushed over from Germany. The Isle of Wight had become almost his second home: indeed, he had so dominated the Cowes yachting seasons that his uncle sardonically called him "the Boss of Cowes".

Now, as his grandmother breathed her last, he "bossed the show", according to his uncle who, while he prayed at his mother's bedside, was mortified to see Willy holding the Queen in his arms, in which she died.

The new King Edward VII and his nephew then laid her in her coffin, wrapped in her wedding veil.

This was perhaps the last time they would be together for some time. They never liked each other. The new King had often slapped Willy, when he was still young, for being a nuisance.

Within a quarter of an hour King Edward telegraphed the news to the Lord Mayor of London. It is almost impossible now to realize the shock caused to the country by the Queen's death. She had been Sovereign so long that thousands of her subjects had been born, grown up, got married and died without having known any other monarch. People had taken her for granted so very much that they expected her to live for ever.

Hers was a most magnificent funeral. They took her little body from her island home on a day of glittering frost. The coffin looked tiny as it was borne along, with the Crown of England twinkling on it.

The weather was so bitter that when they got the coffin to the gun-carriage that was waiting to take her to the station the horses took fright on the slippery road and had to be unharnessed because it was impossible to quieten them.

In the end the bluejackets, hand-picked from among the sailors of the Queen's proud and powerful Navy, brought her body to the station, and the crowned heads of Europe lined up behind the coffin in a memorable cavalcade.

She was laid to rest at Frogmore by the side of the Prince Consort. She had rejoined The Beloved One at last.

12

The Throne at Last

This was the end of an era which had lasted far too long, for during her last years there was very little that the Queen could do, and she would never give way to her son.

Now he had come to the throne – perhaps too late. He hoped not!

There was never any guarantee that Edward and Alexandra would succeed to the throne. As I have shown, their expectation of ever wearing the crown was almost destroyed by their serious illnesses when they were Prince and Princess of Wales and by the assassination attempt at Brussels which so very nearly succeeded.

So there was no time to lose, and Edward started immediately to put in hand those things which he had always wanted to do.

He was enchanted to open dusty and neglected Buckingham Palace properly and to move in there, while provision was made for his surviving son George, Duke of York, now also automatically Duke of Cornwall (though he was not created Prince of Wales until the King celebrated his sixtieth birthday on 9th November 1901), to take over Marlborough House.

The King was delighted to see the royal standard flying over Buckingham Palace again to indicate that the Sovereign was in residence. But there was a lot to be done there first.

"It's in a most ghastly state of disrepair," he said, "and it simply must be cleaned up properly in time for the coronation."

While the late Queen lived few people ever saw inside her private apartments either at the palace or at Windsor. The new Queen Alexandra was not one of the few. One of the first things she saw at Windsor Castle was a marble effigy of Princess Elizabeth of Clarence, the baby daughter of King William IV and Queen Adelaide, who would have reigned as Queen Elizabeth II had she survived, but she died in infancy.

"Whoever could that child have been?" asked the Queen.

The King replied: "If that child had lived, my dear, you and I would not have been here now."

At fifty-six Queen Alexandra was still one of the most beautiful women of her day, outshining in looks and grooming many of the King's favourite ladies, past or present. Yet she refused to be addressed as "Your Majesty" until after Queen Victoria's funeral. She had lived for forty years under the influence of that awesome lady, and even though she was dead Alexandra still remembered her with reverence.

Among the "baubles" which the King cleared out of the castle were the relics of one person who had never been very kind to him – John Brown, the former Highland ghillie who had been Victoria's devoted companion for her years of widowhood and had kept the Heir to the Throne at arm's length. Edward found a lot of pictures, photographs, busts and statues of this strange person whom he believed had exerted an unhealthy influence on his mother.

He smashed up the frames and trampled every John Brown memorial into the dust. It gave him the deepest pleasure!

Those early days were very bustling ones. Wilhelm stayed on in England for the Queen's funeral on 4th February. He behaved very well, and was so charming to everyone that the King – who usually suspected him of ulterior motives, and most often was right – was quite deceived. He made his nephew an honorary field marshal and invested him with the Order of the Garter.

The King even wrote to his sister Vicky, the Dowager Empress Frederick, who was suffering from incurable cancer and was much too unwell to travel to London, praising Willy for his devotion and his kindness which, he said, had greatly touched him. He also asked his dying sister's blessing "to fulfil my arduous and onerous duties."

It was not until eleven days after the funeral that the new monarchs made their first public appearance, and that was at the State Opening of Parliament, and soon after the Edward left in the *Victoria and Albert* to see his sister in Germany. It was an agonizing meeting for them both, but there was one little light incident.

For three nights running, the King discovered, *thirteen* people had sat down to dinner. He was a very superstitious man (his valet was even forbidden to turn his mattress on a Friday), and the discovery upset him ... until he was reminded that one of the guests was Princess Charles of Hesse and that she was expecting a baby, so really there had been *fourteen* at table all the time!

On his return, while Buckingham Palace was being refurbished, he continued to live at Marlborough House, but he started the habit of dining out in the homes of some of his subjects in London. No Sovereign had done that since George IV. People in Society were delighted to see the tradition revived.

One of the first with whom he dined in this way was Alice Keppel, who was to remain his dear friend and comforter to the end of his days.

But the King worked hard at *being* a king, for in his heart he knew that he would have very little time, and there was much to put straight before he followed his ancestors to the vaults at Windsor. He had always been an extremely energetic worker, and at sixty he was still full of boyish curiosity and youthful zest and enthusiasm, although his constant eating and drinking and smoking made inroads into his robust constitution. "Tum Tum" was becoming very portly indeed, but it was useless for his medical men to advise him to cut down on his eating.

One of his first tasks was to sign more than six thousand

military commissions. These had fallen hopelessly behind during the last phase of Queen Victoria's life, and the backlog had been increased by the addition of commissions granted as a result of the war in South Africa.

In the end he had to use a rubber stamp and become more selective about which commissions he signed with his own hand. It had been much the same for William IV when *he* came to the throne and found that his brother George IV had left him a huge legacy of State documents and other papers to be signed, until his hand was red and swollen and had to be poulticed.

Edward's coming to the throne with his lovely wife brought a new thrill to the country, and people got much joy out of seeing the King and Queen once again drive out through the palace gates, where there was always a crowd to cheer and wave at them.

The King went everywhere and was always very friendly to people. In addition he supervised detailed arrangements for the coronation, which was fixed for 26th June 1902.

There had been no coronation for nearly two-thirds of a century – and this was to be a very special one because since Victoria herself had been crowned Queen she had also become Empress of India. So Edward's crowing was the first directly involving the British Empire.

Overseas potentates, Indian princes and many foreign royalties had already begun to arrive in London when the King went down to Windsor for Ascot Week. The nation was now out of mourning for the Queen and ready for the coronation, was in a gay mood, with the stands going up along the coronation route in London, and everything prepared. Then came rumours that the King was unwell. They proved to be only too well-founded.

Twelve days before the great Abbey ceremony he was thought to be "ill with a severe chill". Even then he refused to shirk any of the details of planning for the coronation in which he was so deeply immersed, and he was not only determined to keep on supervising various renovations at Buckingham

Palace and Windsor Castle, but he was also studying designs for a new livery for his servants!

The King reluctantly agreed to be put on a milk diet, but as the days passed and he got no better it was given out falsely that he was suffering only from a severe attack of lumbago. That was done to allay public alarm and, of course, the King stubbornly refused to back down on anything.

He sent the Queen to Ascot. She left him very unwillingly, but it was necessary to give the impression that all was well, except for the "lumbago". It was "business as usual" – and the King declared that he would attend his coronation even if he dropped dead.

The thought of disappointing so many people simply appalled him, but it was no use. He returned to Buckingham Palace three days before the coronation, and after a medical examination he was solemnly informed by his physician, Sir Francis Laking, that he had appendicitis and that unless an operation was performed without delay the consequences could be fatal.

Still the King, in great pain and suffering much mental anguish as well, insisted that the coronation must go on.

"Afterwards you may cut me in two," he said, "but I can't – I *won't* – disappoint the people!"

The Serjeant-Surgeon, Sir Edward Treves, replied gently that unless the King submitted to surgery immediately he would arrive at Westminster Abbey in his coffin.

The pain was now so intense that the King could hardly bear it. It is reported that he said: "If this goes on I shall abdicate." In addition, the noise made by the carpenters erecting the wooden stands outside the palace made things worse.

So the hammering was stopped while Treves and his assistants prepared to operate. Crowds now stood around the palace railings waiting silently for news. Edward had waited *so* long to reign over them, and now the awful horror came that there was something really wrong, and perhaps he was going to die before he could be crowned!

After Treves's first visit a bulletin was issued, and this time it showed what was really the matter.

An operation for appendicitis was almost new in medical history, and the bulletin stated that he was to undergo surgery at once. It was such a dangerous proceeding that before the final decision was taken two other famous medical men, Lord Lister and Sir Thomas Smith, were called into consultation.

Treves performed the operation in forty minutes. Meanwhile the crowd outside the palace had swelled, and the numbers did not begin to diminish until a notice was brought out and hung on the railings saying that the King had had his operation and, although he was not yet conscious, all was well.

The bulletin was signed by Lord Lister, Sir Francis Laking (who had first warned the King of peritonitis complications), Sir Thomas Barlow, Sir Thomas Smith, and Sir Frederick Treves. It was received by the crowd in unbroken silence, as had been requested, as any noise might have disturbed the sleeping patient.

A coronation dress rehearsal was at that moment taking place at the abbey: on the orders of the Bishop of London it was turned into a service of intercession.

Presumably the King had been thinking of what would happen if he died, for on coming out of the chloroform he asked for his son, George.

By 5th July the world knew that His Majesty was out of danger; it was a tremendous relief. He made the most miraculous recovery, and ten days later he was moved to the royal yacht. Every phase of the journey to the Isle of Wight was personally supervised by Queen Alexandra, whose gaiety and apparent light-heartedness aboard the yacht did more to restore her husband to health than any diet, doctor or nurse.

The coronation took place in August, by which time many of the overseas guests had returned home. The ceremony was curtailed to spare the King, but he was in great good humour, and before he left the palace for the abbey he put on his robes to show his grandchildren, saying: "Am I not a funny-looking old man?"

As for Queen Alexandra, she was hailed as the most beautiful Consort who had ever entered the abbey. And she was attended by four of the loveliest women in England.

Princess Marie Louise recalled that the Queen was a little dismayed because "a drop of the Holy Oil with which she had been anointed had trickled down on to her dear little nose, fear of irreverence preventing her, as she told me, from using her handkerchief!"

Soon after the coronation the King arranged to meet the Kaiser in Berlin. His sister Vicky, the Kaiser's mother, had died in August after much suffering, and Edward and Alexandra attended her funeral. Then the King had talks with his nephew about Anglo-German relations. But nothing came of them, as it was quite clear that public opinion both in Britain and in Germany was opposed to any kind of alliance.

In November 1902 the Kaiser visited Sandringham, for the last time, as things turned out. The King considered that he had been "lucky" to get safely over his operation – I think he was right – and he wanted to establish the rest of his life in the way that he always wanted most.

His idea was to achieve lasting security for his country because he had a strong premonition that war lay ahead. He believed that the epoch of great nations living together, as we had done for so many years, was changing and that something ought to be done to establish the peace which he wanted so much.

But Willy at Sandringham proved even more insufferable than ever, and constantly irritated his uncle. Queen Alexandra had to draw hugely on her reserves of tact and diplomacy to cool tempers, although the King was exasperated beyond measure when the Kaiser went for a drive in one of Edward's prized motor-cars and then told him that he was using the wrong petrol. That was bad enough, but the Kaiser sent to Germany for potato spirit, which he assured the King was much better, and that made things *worse*!

So on that occasion, too, nothing came of efforts to get Germany to share in the idea of universal peace.

This Sandringham visit marked an important stage in the career of Edward the Peacemaker. For years he had been overshadowed by the young Kaiser's presumption of power, by his jaunty expeditions to various countries proclaiming the growing might of the German Empire, an empire which he had inherited following the defeat of France in the time of his grandfather.

Now, as King at last, it was Edward's turn. No sooner had Willy departed for home – "Thank God!" exclaimed King Edward when he left Portsmouth – than he went ahead with a plan which had been fermenting for some time. This was to make a royal grand tour of Europe in the spring of 1903. That decision was to be the forerunner of a turning-point in human affairs.

The King made this a personal tour: he refused to be accompanied by any Cabinet Minister, though normally he would have been expected to take the Foreign Secretary, Lord Lansdowne, with him. In addition, he made all the arrangements himself.

The tour started off in Portugal. Meanwhile he had notified President Loubet of France that he would be more than pleased to visit Paris on his way home. His advisers shrank back from such a step, for relations with France – arising partly out of the celebrated Fashoda incident – were far from cordial.

Edward also brushed aside objections to his calling upon the aged Pope Leo XIII in Rome: it was feared that such a visit might upset the Irish Protestants. But the King told his advisers not to be absurd, and he was proved right. That visit was a minor triumph.

In Paris, where he arrived on May Day, the King to his surprise received a warmer welcome than he had expected. Although the Paris crowds were at first rather cool, and cheered the Boers and shouted "Vive Fashoda!" – and even gave three cheers for Joan of Arc – as the royal procession made its way up the Champs Elysées the King's friendliness and the warmth of his personality melted French hearts, especially after he had kissed the hand of a famous French actress and paid her a pretty compliment, which was taken up by the French Press and repeated everywhere.

Of course he went to the races at Longchamps, and by the time he had taken his seat at the Opera the French crowds were greeting him with shouts of "Good old Teddy!" After that it was "Vive Edouard!" all the way.

13
The 'Entente Cordiale'

The European tour lasted five weeks. When Edward reached home on 5th May the British Government and people sensed that the King, who saw a good deal further ahead than some of his advisers, had made a significant contribution to the cause of peace on which he had set his sights.

Thus was *L'Entente Cordiale* born. I suppose that this was what saved the situation when war came after his death and Europe was plunged into battle by the Kaiser's Germany.

"France must be always our friend," was what he said.

In Paris he had made a most magnificent speech. He was rather good at speech-making – I think this gift had always made his mother jealous, for her speeches were not particularly great. He said: "The days of conflict between our two countries are, I trust, happily over, and I hope that future historians, in alluding to Anglo-French relations, may be able to record only our friendly rivalry in the field of commerce and industrial developments. In the future, as in the past, we hope for a peaceful progress and civilization, and some of all that is best."

Then, in a voice full of emotion: "A divine Providence has designed that France should be our nearest neighbour and, I hope, always a dear friend."

This brought a most vigorous response, which proved that he was, after all, dearly loved in France and that the French trusted him, whatever they felt about his Government. He most certainly wanted to be a good neighbour, and now he was laying the foundation stone of *L'Entente Cordiale*.

Yet the King was ahead of public opinion in his own country. The *entente* was distrusted, largely because for centuries France had been the enemy of Britain. But an understanding with Russia, which was also reached at this time, was also disliked by the people. The fact is, no doubt, that the British people did not like being mixed up with *foreigners*!

As his official biographer has said, the King's governments "reaped quite a useful harvest from the goodwill and confidence which he inspired" – and this was underlined when the French President paid a return State visit to London. President Loubet was received most loyally with a tremendous show of flags, while huge crowds gathered in the streets to cheer him through the city. Soldiers lined the routes and the crowd was high-spirited, for we were now whispering about something which was to be called *L'Entente Cordiale* which we hoped would mean security for us for as far as we could see ahead.

Now it seemed that England had come right royally out of the gloom cast by the Victorian era, and into the sunlight. The King believed in shows and was everywhere among his subjects. "I owe this to my people," he said. Débutantes lined up at the palace to curtsy to the Sovereign and his Consort. Trade improved. It looked like being a happier and more delightful world in which to live.

There was great rejoicing when the Anglo-French agreement was signed in London in 1904 by Lord Lansdowne and M. Paul Cambon (he lasted as French ambassador in London from 1898 to 1920). It was a superb move towards peace, and it came in the year of the first Empire Day – 24th May, the anniversary of Queen Victoria's birth in 1819 – and was so significant as a contribution to the permanent peace that this great King so desired to bring to the world.

Naturally, the creation of a new understanding with France, which led to talks between the British and French military staffs, caused no joy in Germany.

The King was very worried about the German reaction and proposed a visit to Berlin, but the Kaiser instead invited him to meet him aboard the imperial yacht *Hohenzollern* at Kiel. Wilhelm's real motive was to show off the might of the German Navy.

It seemed that on this visit the Kaiser warmed towards his uncle in a new way, and the King hoped that the tide was turning. He bore a sense of resentment that his favourite sister had been so unhappy in Germany, but, as he told himself, this was not the time for that sort of thing. He wanted peace for the world.

His nephew made a glowing speech. He said:

"For the first time I welcome Your Majesty on board a German ship-of-war. May our two flags fly beside each other to the most distant time, as they fly together for the maintenance of peace and for the well-being not only of our two countries but also of the world."

One wonders if the King believed him, for recent years had widened the breach with the nephew whom he had once spoken of as "that brat". But both of them made amiable speeches at that time, and it looked as if the outcome would be promising.

In the event, however, the King did not endear himself to the Emperor by scoffing at Wilhelm's warning that a Japanese victory over Russia – the two countries were then at war – would destroy world peace. The Kaiser had an obsession about "the Yellow Peril".

From that time, indeed, the Kaiser and his British relations drifted further apart. One day in October 1904 the Russian Baltic Fleet shelled some Hull trawlers off the Dogger Bank, believing them to be Japanese gunboats! Wilhelm reacted violently to this incident, threatening to occupy Denmark and close the Kattegat if the British Fleet stormed into the Baltic. This upset Queen Alexandra, who had never forgiven Germany for the earlier attack on her native land, or the Kaiser for his ill-treatment of his mother.

Then Willy tried to interfere with Edward's attempts to get

Prince Charles of Denmark elevated to the throne of Norway with his daughter Maud as Queen. The Kaiser failed, Charles succeeded as King Haakon, but the dispute left scars.

King Edward believed in placing English princesses judicially and so ensuring peace with a country, or so he hoped, and Princess Margaret of Connaught, his brother's daughter, married the Crown Prince Gustav of Sweden and later became Queen. Europe was particularly thrilled by this wedding, for when the young girl entered the Swedish cathedral she carried marguerites in her arms, and all those English bridesmaids following her were carrying posies of these lovely flowers, too.

It was later in the reign when young King Alfonso XIII of Spain came to visit the Court in search of a bride. A big ball was arranged for him at Buckingham Palace. The King was a great match-maker and had hoped that the second daughter of the Duke of Connaught, Princess Patricia, would become Queen of Spain, but she failed to turn up at the ball! It so happened that the daughter of Queen Victoria's youngest and favourite child, Princess Beatrice, was there. This young lady, Princess Ena of Battenberg, fell in love with Alfonso at first sight. They were married.

Edward VII worked hard for his country, placing his princesses on suitable thrones, but all the time he knew that he would never live long enough and he dreaded what would happen if he had not finally settled things before he himself went.

In January 1906 old King Christian of Denmark died. His departure from the European stage on which he had played a secondary but important part for so many years deeply distressed Queen Alexandra. The Christian family had never been rich, but they were homely, influential, and were extremely fond of one another. His death upset King Edward, too.

"I hate to see a woman crying," he said.

The royal doctors warned Edward against over-work, but

nothing stopped him. He had got to make sure of peace, and he did not trust his nephew in Germany; he had always said so! He had, of course, new designs for ships and for guns, for one had to be prepared even if one fought for peace, and a lasting peace was what he prayed for.

Queen Alexandra was still a beautiful woman; though she aged she showed no sign of it. But she *was* deafer, though she would not admit this – which at times could be trying! And her growing unpunctuality exasperated the King.

Make-up had come into fashion (hitherto it had been rather thrust aside), but now all women used powder, though a lipstick would have been a bit much. Alexandra dressed well and held herself beautifully, and some said that her daughters looked to be older than she did!

But time was running out for the King and for Europe. Nobody realized this more than Edward, whose doctors constantly warned him not to do too much. But he was always restless in the cause of peace at home and abroad, and he tried hard to win over not only France but also Russia, and even the United States, to the British point of view.

In July 1905 the Czar of Russia, Nicholas II, who was Edward's nephew through Alexandra's sister Dagmar, met the German Emperor aboard the *Hohenzollern* and the Russian imperial yacht *Standart* off Viborg – an occasion made memorable by Wilhelm's sharp attack on Edward VII as the greatest "mischief-maker" in the world and a dangerous and insincere "arch-intriguer".

The Czar foolishly signed a treaty with Germany without quite seeing its implications, but he afterwards repudiated it. The Kaiser then characteristically turned on him, saying that while he was not exactly treacherous he was "weak" – and that weakness was as bad as treachery!

About two years later, in June 1908, the King and Queen arranged a family reunion with Nicholas and the Czarina – the former Princess Alix ('Alicky') of Hesse – aboard the yachts *Victoria and Albert* and *Standart* at Reval. Wilhelm exploded, declaring that "Edward aims at war", which could not have been more wrong.

On the way home the *Victoria and Albert* passed through the Kiel Canal, and Wilhelm ordered a regiment of dragoons to salute the British monarchs as it passed. Alexandra told her servants to pull down the blinds of her cabin windows in order to shut out the hateful sight. For Wilhelm it was a profound humiliation.

14

Crisis-and Death

The King was now worried about the political outlook at home. Mr Lloyd George was unlike the King in outlook, and he had become Chancellor of the Exchequer. This man had a glib tongue and a ready wit, which he turned on the House of Lords, observing among other things that "a fully-equipped Duke cost as much to keep up as two Dreadnoughts".

The King protested that he thought this campaign against the Lords was wrong, although for a long time he had considered that a modest reform of the structure of the Upper Chamber might be useful.

At this time, in 1909, he had been on the throne for eight years and his health was giving rise to anxiety. Mr Campbell-Bannerman, the Liberal Prime Minister, had died – he collapsed after making a gruelling speech at Bristol – and had been replaced by Mr Asquith, to whom the King complained that Lloyd George was trying to drag the crown into the argument, asking whether the country should be governed by the King and the peers or the King and his elected Commons. It was then that the King came forward (for he had that right) and insisted that his name should be kept out of party politics.

Unfortunately, Mr Asquith found it hard to keep his Ministers in order, as his predecessor had contrived to do, and now the whole aspect of Parliament was disturbing to the King.

He was alarmed about the state of Europe. He pointed out that the growth and development of implements of war showed only too clearly that there could be war in Europe which would be disastrous. One could win it, but too many of our attempts towards progress would be halted or shattered in the process, thousands of hearts broken, and the whole peace of the world endangered.

He was so right, but at the time nobody believed him. Now came this question of "The People's Budget" to plague him.

It was on 26th May 1909 – the birthday of the Prince of Wales – that he won his third Derby (his first as King), this time with *Minoru*. The Epsom racegoers burst into "God Save the King" and shouted "Good old Teddy!" and "Hurrah for Teddy boy!"

When he returned to Epsom next day someone shouted: "Now, King, you've won the Derby – go back home and dissolve this —— Parliament!"

He laughed at the time, but "The People's Budget", presented by Lloyd George the week before, caused him deep concern, not because of the social reforms which it introduced (modest by modern standards, but regarded as the end of the world by some people in high places), but also because it threatened to cause a clash between the Lords and the Commons.

In those days, of course, the Lords could block any financial measure, but they were no longer permitted to do this after that great constitutional issue had been resolved – but by then the King was dead.

The King also strongly resented the powerful language used by Lloyd George and other reforming Ministers in the course of the Budget campaign. Violent words were also used by the Unionist opposition.

In the end the Lords threw out the Budget, a general election was called, and the country was precipitated into a constitutional crisis such as it had not known since the Reform Bill controversy of the early years of William IV.

The outcome of this parliamentary struggle – Peers versus People, as the Liberals called it – has passed into history. But the thought that he might be called upon to create enough new peers to push the Budget and its enacting Finance Bill through the Lords haunted the King. The dispute was inherited by his son when he became George V, and the subsequent passage of the Parliament Act of 1911 severely limited the powers of the House of Lords.

For by the beginning of 1910 the King was obviously in failing health. He had been travelling about far too much. Again and yet again his doctors told him the strain was too great. But he was so eager to restore stability at home and establish peace abroad that he did not seem to mind if he killed himself with work in the process provided he stood some chance of success.

In the previous spring the House of Commons had been warned that by 1912 Germany might possess twenty-one Dreadnoughts to Great Britain's twenty, and this was not good. The insistence on further armaments – and they were most necessary at this time to combat Germany's growing strength – had sent up the income tax, and this irritated everybody.

The King himself was intensely popular, and he was trying to act helpfully. He was a man with the wide outlook of his father, and he often encouraged other forms of the Christian faith. Queen Alexandra had placed a memorial in Notre Dame Cathedral in Paris in gratitude for his recovery from appendicitis, and he himself had lit a candle at the shrine of Our Lady of Lourdes, which was still alight after he who had lit it had gone to his fathers.

In one last despairing effort to patch up the peace with the Kaiser, the King and Queen paid a State visit to Berlin, but the whole thing turned out to be a disaster.

The royal visitors were dismayed by Wilhelm's ostentatious display of militarism, and the Germans greeted them coolly.

At a British embassy dinner before the visit ended the guests were thrown into consternation when the King was suddenly seized with a spasm of coughing. He went black in the face as he tried to get back his breath. Alexandra, rising quickly to the emergency, ordered everyone from the room except a doctor. When the guests returned they found the poor King sitting defiantly smoking a cigar but with his collar sadly crumpled after the doctor's heroic efforts to restore his breathing. It was a close thing.

During 1909 the King crossed the Channel six times. On one occasion he went to his favourite Marienbad in what was then called Bohemia. While there he consulted a German doctor whom he knew and liked. The celebrated Dr Ott told him that he was wonderfully well for his years. This cheered the King greatly, especially when the specialist added that in his opinion he had the mental concentration of a man half his years. This did help him.

"I shall remember what you have said," he told the doctor.

One of his engagements at home, when he was feeling rather restless, was at West Dean Park, near Chichester, of which he was very fond. He was staying with Mr and Mrs Willy James, who were very great friends of his.

Whilst he was there he opened the Institute of Tuberculosis in Montreal by merely pressing a button. This marvel of remote control was something quite new and delighted him because it set the world talking about his country, and about him as a most go-ahead man with the same scientific outlook as his distinguished father, and as a man who had hated living in a rut and who wanted his country to remain in the van as a country of progress. But the Queen was very concerned about him. He was never happy unless he was doing far too much, she complained.

On a visit to Malta he stayed with his brother the Duke of Connaught, who was not only High Commissioner but also Commander-in-Chief of all British garrisons in and around the Mediterranean. Unhappily, the King and his brother had a difference about defence policy in that region, and the Duke asked to be relieved of his duties. In this dispute Kitchener sided with the Duke, and in the end the King generously agreed that he had been wrong, and he made it up with his brother, who later was sent to Ottawa as Governor-General of Canada.

But the King was usually right in large affairs. During this Mediterranean visit he entertained the King and Queen of Italy to dinner and made a speech proposing an Anglo-Italian alliance. This was described by Asquith as "tactless". But in view of what happened afterwards, when Italy came into the Great War on the side of the Western allies, who could say that once again the King had not been right in foreseeing the shape of things to come?

So far as his health was concerned, the King was quite agreeable – though reluctant – to stay in bed when he was ill, but the moment he felt better he got up sooner than the doctors considered to be wise, and he was out and about again before he should have been.

A long rest was prescribed for him, but he absolutely refused to take it, though they told him that it was the only thing that would put him back on his feet.

Queen Alexandra wanted him to go on a cruise in the new royal yacht, *Alexandra*. But he preferred to go to Biarritz. Since his later years as Prince of Wales he had liked to go to Paris and then spend a few weeks at the famous resort in the South-West.

Realizing how much good Biarritz did for him, his doctors urged him to take a holiday there so as to avoid the sharpness of the March days in England. He felt so well then that the night before he left he gave a dinner party at the palace and took his fill of a great nine-course meal. Next day in Paris he caught a chill, and when he reached Biarritz he collapsed and was confined to his hotel room, though he refused to take to his bed.

One of his visitors was Mrs Keppel. Meanwhile Queen Alexandra was urging him to leave "horrid" Biarritz and join her on the yacht. That was "quite out of the question", said the King, because he might have to get back to London in a hurry, as the constitutional brawl over the Parliament Bill was coming to the boil.

The King seemed better when he returned to London in

that April of 1910. He attended a performance of *Siegfried* at Covent Garden at the end of the month. When he entered the royal box he was given a most tremendous ovation, the whole house rising to cheer him. That, so he said, did more to help him than all the doctor's medicines. Perhaps he had got depressed and was imagining that he was ill when he was not.

Next day he went down to Sandringham before the Queen returned from Greece, where she had been visiting her relations. He felt more than the usual restlessness, but Sandringham was always *home*, he said, and he liked inspecting his pedigree stock and paying visits to old servants who were living on the estate in grace-and-favour houses allotted to them, and who were always enchanted to see him.

The days were bright with the new spring, but there was a cold easterly wind blowing, for the weather was not reliable. He looked forward to 6th May when the Queen would be returning from her cruise and they would be together again. The years of their reign had united them as never before, this bluff, kind-hearted King and his lovely Queen whose beauty and charm had become a legend.

Back in London there were several commitments with which he had to cope, but some of them had to be cancelled because he simply was not feeling well enough to keep them. When the day came for the Queen's return he said he had never looked forward to anything so much in his entire life. But to his horror he found that he had not enough strength to go to the station to meet her, something he had never failed to do before.

The Queen had been in Corfu when she was warned that all was not well with the King. She was appalled, for when he had told her that he "was not very well" she had never thought that it would be as bad as this. Her apprehensions turned to alarm when he failed to appear at the station, and her carriage could not get to Buckingham Palace quickly enough.

She immediately went to his room and was utterly shocked to see how he looked, oh, so changed! His voice, usually strong and sturdy, especially his laugh, was thin and low: at moments it failed him as he struggled for breath. But he was enchanted to see her again, and said that now he would improve, for she was life itself to him.

"Why did you not let me know what was happening?" she asked him, both shocked and bewildered. "You knew that I would have wanted to be with you!"

He did not answer – just a helpless gesture of the hand.

After a light luncheon he had had a severe heart attack which came on while he was playing with his two pet canaries. The Queen was aghast. Why had nobody told her? What a home-coming!

Poor Queen Alexandra, everything had happened with such frightful suddenness and it was quite dreadful for her. She hovered near to him while the doctors tried to save his life, well aware that her presence alone gave him some small comfort and doing everything she could, even concealing her grief lest it worry him.

I imagine that he had known that the end could not be far away for some time now, but he faced up to it with a courage which had always made him so great. He could not hasten things, but he could not deter them either. Death is the last stranger whom all of us have to meet.

As soon as the Queen realized that he was dying – the doctors held out no hope – she did the kindest thing that anyone ever did, for she sent for Mrs Keppel. She knew full well of their great friendship, and she believed that to have her near him now might make things a little easier for him. It was courageous and extremely thoughtful of her, for she herself had always been in love with him all their married life!

He was a man who loved women, all pretty women, and the other loves of his life had either drifted away, or quarrelled with him, but there was this one dear friend, Alice Keppel, to whom he could turn when in trouble. All through their married life Queen Alexandra had acknowledged his flirtations, and had accepted them and glossed over them as being part of his nature. They had never distressed her, nor had she been jealous in any way, though they might have upset some women in similar circumstances. All she wanted was his happiness, for she was deeply fond of him, and had been, from the first moment when they had met in that cathedral, two young people destined to fall in love at first sight.

In the end the news came to the outside world that the Archbishop of Canterbury was with the dying king. There was a terrible sense of personal loss throughout his country! Huge crowds waited in deathly silence round the palace, standing in homage for the passing of one of our greatest monarchs, who, if he had come to the throne before he did, could perhaps have saved us from so much that happened later! He could perhaps have settled a permanent peace for Europe, if only he had had the time. Victoria lived too long, and he did not reign long enough.

The news came as a traumatic shock to the more remote parts of the country, for it was all so sudden, and it came on a May morning when the sunshine was pouring down, the may was in bud in the hedgerows, and nobody had felt that anything really serious was going on.

The news was brought to my mother and myself that the King was dead, and for a short time we simply could not believe it. Then we *had* to believe it. That was, I think, when the greatness of this country suddenly stopped, as perhaps he had known it might do, unless he could get Europe in a better mood before he went.

There was the usual splendid funeral, the lying-in-state, and then travelling through London to Paddington Station, down to Windsor, with the crown of England flashing on the coffin, and the new King George V following him.

It was a very sad procession, for there were many who never realized how great this man had been until they learnt that he had gone. And although the funeral of Queen Victoria had been far more dramatic, somehow for this King there was really deep sorrow, for he was a monarch who had always been the friend of his people.

At Windsor he was buried in the crypt with his forbears.

Somehow one was glad he would not lie in the mortuary chapel at Frogmore with the old Queen and her Prince, for although he had adored his father, he had never really got on with his mother, because of that strange antipathy which she had always felt for his likeness to King George IV. It was most unfair of her, for he was the most charming man, and she must have been the only person in the world who felt that way about him. All of us can be martyrs to a family likeness. He would have been happier if his mother had died, and his father had been left, for he never did get on with his mother from the first time that Mrs Lily had laid him in her arms.

It was a terribly sad procession at Windsor. Immediately behind the coffin stood the small, very slight Queen Alexandra, heavily veiled, and her son, the new King. This was the man who had never wanted to be king, but had sought to stay with the Royal Navy all his life, but the death of his elder brother had brought him to this place.

The widowed Queen would have heard very little of the service, for now she was really very deaf, and perhaps in some ways this was a good thing. Near to her stood her grandsons, and amongst them Kaiser Wilhelm.

For him he must have thought things were working out well. He would never have fought his uncle, he *did* know better than that he might have felt that the new King would be easy meat.

At that very hour he must have known that Germany was arming for war, awaiting the chance, and the moment that it came they *would* take it.

Edward VII was the man who loved peace, and sought to outlaw war, so that it could never happen again. He did not live long enough to do this, perhaps nobody lives long enough for such a noble work, and peace is not easy to establish for ever. He died too soon because he had come to the throne too late.

Queen Alexandra retired to Sandringham, and lived the quiet life there amongst her friends, of whom she had many.

King George V started his reign, knowing that his father had not achieved the permanent peace which he had sought: there simply had not been the time.

All the passing foolishness – the wine, women, and song periods of Edward's life had come because the old Queen would give him nothing to do, but insisted on keeping all government in her own hands when those hands were already too old and too infirm. He was never consulted in anything that she did, and when he was crowned at last it was too late!

Edward the Peacemaker was dead.